DAILY CLOSE-UPS
FOR FALL

Written by Mary Magaldi, Bruce Russell, and Carol Olsgard

Edited by Connie Flesner
Illustrated by Nancee McClure

Cover by Gary Mohrmann

GOOD APPLE, INC.
BOX 299
CARTHAGE, IL 62321-0299

Copyright © Good Apple, Inc., 1984

ISBN No. 0-86653-254-4

Printing No. 9

GOOD APPLE, INC.
BOX 299
CARTHAGE, IL 62321-0299

TABLE OF CONTENTS

INTRODUCTION

Welcome to *Daily Close-Ups for Fall.* We hope you will enjoy these activities to supplement or enhance your daily lessons. This book is divided into three units—September, October and November. Each unit contains twenty-six pages of activities that are based on actual events in history. Each month contains a calendar and a page describing possible ways for the students to use the calendar. You will also find suggestions for using the calendar as a basis for a bulletin board as well as patterns for cutouts that can be decorated and used by the students.

These pages were designed so that you, the teacher, would have an activity for students to do while you are busy taking roll, lunch count, lunch money, etc. Some activities may take the student much longer and perhaps could be used when he/she is finished with other assignments during the day. You, as the teacher, will best know how to use these pages for your students.

I hope you will enjoy this book as much as I have enjoyed editing it. If you like *Daily Close-Ups for Fall,* please note that *Daily Close-Ups for Winter* and *Daily Close-Ups for Spring* are also available from Good Apple.

Good luck and have fun!

Connie Flesner

SEPTEMBER

MS WRIGHT

WHY DOES AUTUMN HAVE TO GO?
The moon is high in the autumn sky
The air is damp and cool,
I sigh and wonder why I have to go to school.
I love the crackly autumn leaves
  rustling in the breeze,
The autumn sun in the autumn sky
  is so wonderful to see.
I look at the pretty autumn leaves
  falling down so slow,
Then I wonder with a sigh—
Why does autumn have to go?

Ewen
Age 9

September

Sunday	Monday	Tuesday	Wednesday	Thursday	Friday	Saturday

A. Run off enough calendars on the opposite page so that each student can have one of his own. You may also want to reproduce the cutouts found at the bottom of this page. The student can use these cutouts as "stickers" for his calendar. If one side of the pattern is put on the fold and the rest is cut out, the student can lift the pattern and write on the inside. These cutout "stickers" can be decorated as the student wishes. The cutout can be taped or glued to the appropriate place on the calendar.

The following activities are suggested uses for the calendar:

1. Each student can use the calendar as a cover for his activity pages. He can glue or tape a cutout on the day that each activity is completed.
2. Each student can keep a daily journal of what he has for breakfast for the month of September. The student can then put a cutout on each day he ate a balanced breakfast. (Hint: This would be an appropriate time to discuss good nutrition with your students.)
3. Another option is to have each student make a September sports booklet of a specific sport or various sports. This booklet can include research on the history, equipment, rules, professional teams, players, etc., of the sports. The calendar can be used as a page for the dates and the scores of the games.

B. Enlarge the calendar (on the opposite page) to design a bulletin board for your classroom. An example is shown above. You may want students to complete ongoing activities to fill in the calendar. One student can be assigned to a specific day of the month. Some suggestions are given below. Enlarge the cutout patterns for students to write down the information they wish to place on the calendar. If one side of the pattern is put on the fold and the rest is cut out, the student can lift the pattern and write on the inside. These cutout "stickers" can be decorated as the student wishes. The cutout can be taped or glued to the appropriate place on the calendar.

1. Have students keep track of the weather for this month. Have a different student record weather information (the temperature, precipitation, wind speed and direction, etc.) for each day of the month.
2. Each day a different student can write down at least one person's birthday for that day of the month. These birthdays can be as general or specific as you decide.
3. Have students record daily sporting events and their scores. If there are no events for that day, students should write down one interesting bit of sports trivia.

3

ACTIVITIES FOR SEPTEMBER

EGGSACTLY WHERE AM I?

September is National Better Breakfast Month. Let us see what eating habits you have. Below write what you had for breakfast.

_____

_____

_____

_____

What four basic food groups should your breakfast include?

1. _____

2. _____

3. _____

4. _____

Eggs are often eaten for breakfast. Below are some egg dishes from all over the world. On the blank beside each, write where the dish would come from.

1. French omelet _____

2. Brazilian coffee souffle _____

3. Fried eggs Romano _____

4. Polish ham and eggs _____

5. Poached eggs topped with grilled Vienna sausages _____

6. Spanish scramble _____

7. Eggs Oriental _____

8. Hoosier egg casserole _____

9. Irish bacon and eggs _____

10. Swedish egg croquettes _____

DON'T BE IN THE DOGHOUSE

The first full week of September is designated as National Dog Week. Below is a list of "dog" words. Match them with their definitions.

_____ dog's life

_____ let sleeping dogs lie

_____ dogbane

_____ dog days

_____ dog-ear

_____ dogfish

_____ dogger

_____ doghole

_____ doghouse

_____ dogtooth

1. dog's shelter

2. a turned down corner of a leaf of a book

3. wretched existence

4. eyetooth

5. leave well enough alone

6. small shark

7. small, miserable place

8. poisonous plant

9. two-masted boat

10. hot, uncomfortable days in July, August

Choose one of the dogs listed below. Write a paragraph on the back about this dog.

Boxer	Pekingese
Chihuahua	Pointer
Cocker Spaniel	Pomeranian
Collie	Pug
Corgi	Retriever
Doberman Pinscher	Saint Bernard
English Setter	Schnauzer
German Shepherd	Sheepdog
Maltese	Siberian Husky
Mastiff	Yorkshire Terrier

If you'd rather, choose a dog of your own to write about.

6

A REST DAY

The first Monday in September is celebrated as Labor Day. This holiday dates back to 1892. Labor means "to work," but most people "rest" on Labor Day.

Below list things you and your family do on Labor Day.

_____

_____

_____

_____

Post offices, banks, schools and many other businesses are closed on Labor Day. List some people and places that would have to be open.

_____

_____

_____

Many towns have a festival celebration over Labor Day. For example, Golden, Illinois, has a Marigold Festival complete with a carnival, softball tournament, tractor pull, and much more. Create your own festival. Write its name and describe it below.

_____

_____

_____

_____

_____

_____

_____

_____

DIAL "O" FOR OPERATOR

On September 1, 1878, the first female telephone operator was hired. Since then women have moved into many new and different jobs once considered only "man's work." Likewise men have begun jobs once considered only "woman's work."

Below describe what you would like to be when you "grow up." Tell *why* you want to have this occupation and *how* you will have to prepare for this career.

_____

_____

_____

_____

_____

_____

_____

_____

_____

_____

_____

_____

_____

_____

_____

_____

_____

_____

_____

_____

_____

_____

... CLOWNING AROUND ...

The first professional school for training potential circus clowns was established September 1, 1968, at Venice, Florida. Students may attend the eight-week free course and learn slaps, falls, juggling, stilt walking, makeup, pantomime, etc.

Read the titles on the clown boxes and make a word bank of at least ten words for each one.

SAD WORDS

SPORTS WORDS

BIG WORDS

HAPPY WORDS

SCARY WORDS

On the back, write an imaginary story about your eight-week stay at the circus clown school. Use at least ten words from the word banks above. Circle them in your story.

EXTRA! EXTRA!

Barney Flaherty became the first newsboy on September 4, 1833, when he answered an advertisement in the newspaper called the *New York Sun.* Barney was then ten years old.

Read the words below which have the word *extra* in them. Look those words up in a dictionary and write the meanings on the lines below.

EXTRA! EXTRA! READ ALL ABOUT IT!

1. *extra*ct _____

_____

2. *extra*ordinary _____

_____

3. *extra*sensory perception _____

_____

4. *extra*vagant _____

_____

5. *extra*curricular _____

_____

6. *extra*dite _____

_____

7. *extra*vaganza _____

_____

8. *extra*terrestrial _____

_____

On the back use numbers 2, 3, 4, and 8 in sentences.

"SAY CHEESE!"

On September 4, 1888, George Eastman of Rochester, New York, patented the first roll film camera. He called it the Kodak No. 1. It used a roll of film of 100 exposures and took a round picture 2½ inches in diameter.

Read the prefixes and their meanings on the roll of film. Use these prefix definitions to help you find the meanings of the words below. Write these on the lines.

mid-
(middle)

il-
(not)

bi-
(two)

fore-
(in front)

auto-
(self)

anti-
(against)

1. bimonthly _____

2. illegal _____

3. antifreeze _____

4. midday _____

5. autograph _____

6. bicycle _____

7. illiterate _____

8. foreground _____

9. autobiography _____

10. midair _____

11. antiwar _____

12. forefront _____

On the back, write at least one more word using each of the prefixes on the roll of film.

FILL 'ER UP!

The first gasoline pump was manufactured in a barn. The first pump and tank were delivered to Jake D. Gumper on September 5, 1885.

Solve the problems below. The first problem under each pump has been done for you.

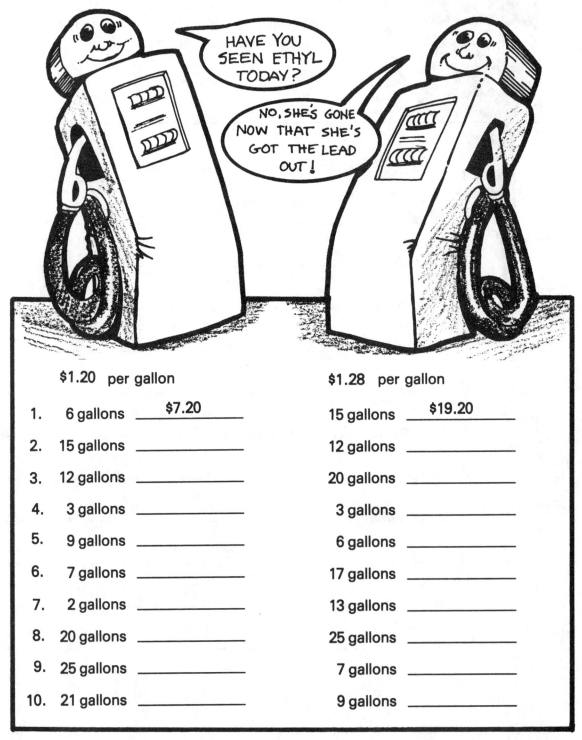

		$1.20 per gallon			$1.28 per gallon
1.	6 gallons	$7.20		15 gallons	$19.20
2.	15 gallons			12 gallons	
3.	12 gallons			20 gallons	
4.	3 gallons			3 gallons	
5.	9 gallons			6 gallons	
6.	7 gallons			17 gallons	
7.	2 gallons			13 gallons	
8.	20 gallons			25 gallons	
9.	25 gallons			7 gallons	
10.	21 gallons			9 gallons	

On the back of this sheet, make up three additional problems for a friend to solve.

12

KEEP ON PEDALING

The first bicycle trip of 100 miles sponsored by a club took place on September 6, 1882. The Boston Bicycle Club of Boston, Massachusetts, sponsored the trip from Worcester, Massachusetts, to Boston. The trip started at 4:38 a.m. and ended at 9:30 p.m. There were stops for food, refreshments, and repairs.

Solve each problem below. Figure the time taken and miles traveled from start to finish. (Traveling speed is 15 miles per hour.)

	Start Time	Miles Traveled	Finish Time
1.	12:00 a.m.	45 miles	3:00 p.m. Time 3 hrs.
2.	10:00 a.m.	___ miles	4:00 p.m. Time ___
3.	11:00 a.m.	___ miles	1:00 p.m. Time ___
4.	9:00 a.m.	___ miles	2:00 p.m. Time ___
5.	8:00 a.m.	___ miles	3:00 p.m. Time ___
6.	7:00 a.m.	___ miles	12:00 a.m. Time ___

FINISH
FINISH
FINISH
FINISH
FINISH
FINISH

A CLAY PIGEON

Have you ever heard of a clay pigeon? The clay pigeon was invented by George Ligowsky of Cincinnati, Ohio. His invention was a clay target used for trapshooting. The flying target was patented on September 7, 1880.

Spell a word on each clay pigeon below. Start with the letter in the middle. Working outward, pick one letter from each ring so that you end up with a four-letter word. Write the word below the clay pigeon. Give yourself points for each word from each target. Some targets are worth more points for each word. Add the points all together and put the total at the bottom.

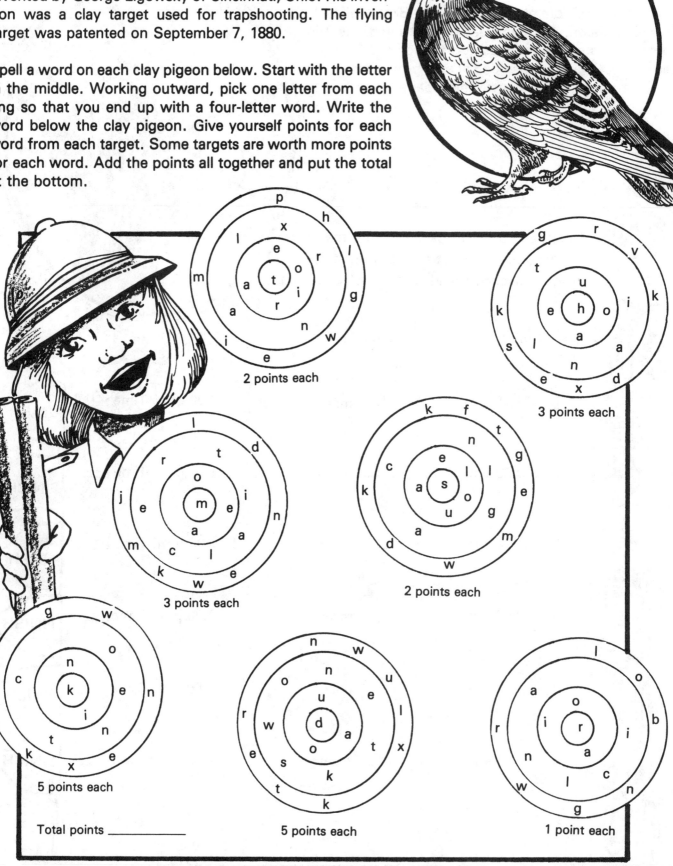

2 points each

3 points each

3 points each

2 points each

5 points each

5 points each

1 point each

Total points _____

14

A RIDE IN RHODE ISLAND

The first automobile race on a track was held September 7, 1896, in Cranston, Rhode Island. Six gasoline and two electric automobiles raced. The winning driver was A. H. Whiting and his approximate speed was 24 mph.

The chart below shows some winning speeds for the Indianapolis 500. Use the chart to answer the questions.

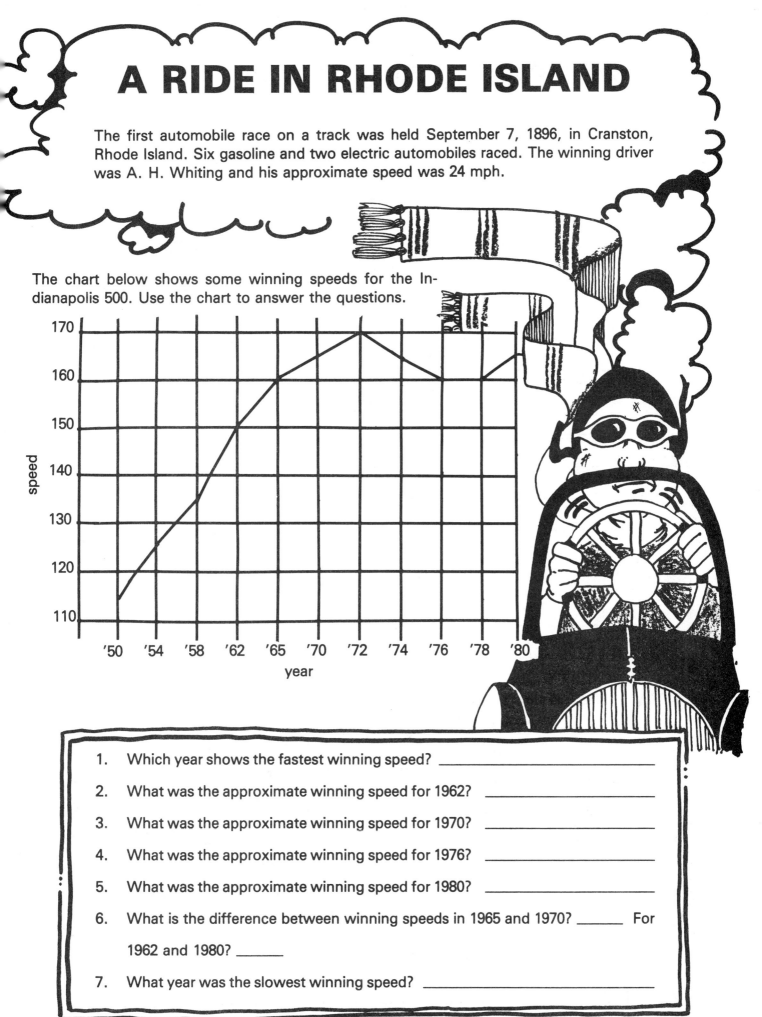

1. Which year shows the fastest winning speed? _____

2. What was the approximate winning speed for 1962? _____

3. What was the approximate winning speed for 1970? _____

4. What was the approximate winning speed for 1976? _____

5. What was the approximate winning speed for 1980? _____

6. What is the difference between winning speeds in 1965 and 1970? _____ For 1962 and 1980? _____

7. What year was the slowest winning speed? _____

I PLEDGE ALLEGIANCE . . .

The Pledge of Allegiance was first read on September 8, 1892. It seems natural to recite the pledge every morning, but can you write it? Write as much of it as you can below.

✶✶✶✶✶✶✶✶✶✶✶✶✶✶✶✶✶✶✶✶✶✶✶✶✶✶✶✶✶✶✶✶✶✶✶✶✶✶

_____

_____

_____

_____

_____

_____

_____

_____

_____

_____

_____

✶✶✶✶✶✶✶✶✶✶✶✶✶✶✶✶✶✶✶✶✶✶✶✶✶✶✶✶✶✶✶✶✶✶✶✶✶✶

CALIFORNIA, HERE WE COME

California became the 31st state on September 9, 1850. California has more people than any other state. Many visitors and new residents are attracted by California's way of life. The warm, dry climate of Southern California permits lightweight clothing and outdoor recreation almost all year round.

A noun is a name of a person, place, or thing. California is a noun because it is the name of a place. Write a noun for each of the letters in the word, California.

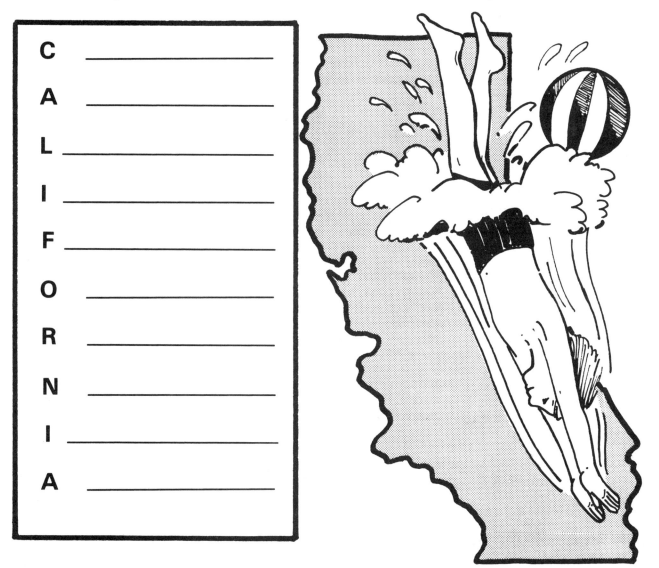

C _____

A _____

L _____

I _____

F _____

O _____

R _____

N _____

I _____

A _____

On the back of this sheet, write three sentences using three nouns you wrote.

THE LOG ROLLED OVER

The first Log Rolling (birling) National Championship was held September 9, 1898, at Omaha, Nebraska, on Lumberman's Day. There were six entries trying to keep their balance while rotating the logs rapidly. The winner was Tom Fleming of Eau Claire, Wisconsin.

Read the sentences on the logs below. These are idiomatic expressions. Spin them around in your head, and write the real meaning of each idiom on the given line. The first one is done for you.

He's in the doghouse now!

1. He is in trouble now!

Don't get your dander up!

7. _____

Are you getting cold feet?

2. _____

Keep a stiff upper lip.

8. _____

She blew her stack!

3. _____

Hold your horses!

He is like a bull in a china shop.

9. _____

Is Dad ever in the dumps!

4. _____

10. _____

He is a pain in the neck!

He lost his shirt on that deal!

5. _____

11. _____

I'm just as fit as a fiddle!

Don't cry over spilt milk.

6. _____

On the back make a picture of one of the sentences above as if you took the meaning literally.

12. _____

STAR-SPANGLED WORDS

Francis Scott Key wrote our national anthem, "The Star-Spangled Banner," on September 13, 1814. He wrote these words while a prisoner on a British warship during the British attack on Fort McHenry in Baltimore, Maryland.

Read the words in the stars below. Look each word up in a dictionary and write the meaning for how it is used in "The Star-Spangled Banner" on the lines below.

1. gleaming

2. perilous

3. twilight

4. hailed

5. gallantly

6. spangled

7. banner

8. ramparts

9. glare

10. streaming

19

A HERSHEY CRUNCH

September 13, 1847, is the day that Milton Hershey was born. He is famous for Hershey's chocolate candy.

Below list some of your favorite candy bars.

_____

_____

_____

_____

Imagine that you are making a new candy bar. Describe it below and make up a name for it. Write it below, also.

_____

_____

_____

_____

_____

M & M's are a type of candy. Below are a few "M & M words." These are words with two M's. See if you can think of more. Write them below.

ammonia	drummer	immediately	scrimmage
brimming	glimmer	plummet	trimmed
common	hammer	rummage	yammer

_____

_____

_____

_____

IT'S A BABY AND ANOTHER . . . AND ANOTHER . . . AND ANOTHER . . .

The first surviving set of quintuplets in America was born on September 14, 1963. Since then many other sets of five children have been born.

A family of quintuplets could be a basketball team. Two sets of quintuplets could be a slow-pitch softball team. Below list other things this instant "team" could do.

_____

_____

_____

_____

_____

_____

_____

_____

_____

The new large family will also have supply difficulties. Help them solve the following problems:

1. Each child needs two sets of diaper pins. How many diaper pins is that? _____

2. Each child needs twelve diapers. How many diapers is that? _____

3. Each child needs one bed. How many beds is that if the parents need one, too? _____

4. Each child needs four bottles. How many bottles are needed all together? _____

5. Each baby wants two rattles. How many rattles do they need? _____

SEWING AROUND

Elias Howe, Jr., received the patent for the first workable sewing machine on September 16, 1846. The first thing he did was to make two suits to demonstrate how strong the machine stitched.

Look at the stitches below. Begin on the star and write each third letter on the lines below in order. If done correctly, the puzzle will tell who eventually marketed this sewing machine. Don't forget to count the star when you go around the second and third times.

___ ___ ___ ___

___ ___ ___ ___ ___ ___

___ ___ ___ ___ ___ ___ ___

___ ___ ___ ___ ___ ___

___ ___ ___ ___ ___ ___ ___ ___

___ ___ ___ ___ ___ ___ ___

On the back make a puzzle for the saying "A stitch in time saves nine" and give it to a friend to do.

CONSTITUTION WEEK

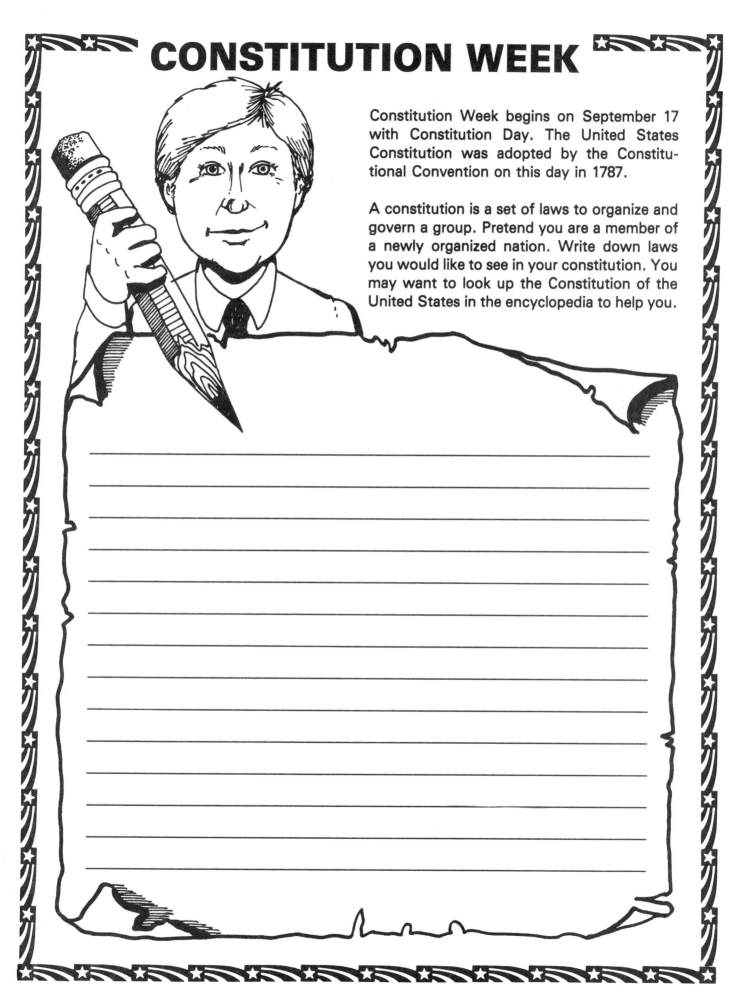

Constitution Week begins on September 17 with Constitution Day. The United States Constitution was adopted by the Constitutional Convention on this day in 1787.

A constitution is a set of laws to organize and govern a group. Pretend you are a member of a newly organized nation. Write down laws you would like to see in your constitution. You may want to look up the Constitution of the United States in the encyclopedia to help you.

SPRINKLE, SPRINKLE

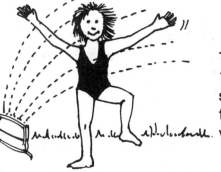

The first sprinkler system patent was granted on September 17, 1872, to Philip W. Pratt of Abington, Massachusetts. This system was set up by means of a valve to which cords and fuses were attached. When the cords and fuses melted, the valve opened, releasing a stream of water.

Read the sentences below. See if you can "sprinkle" each sentence with proper adjectives and adverbs to make them more interesting. Write these on the sprinkle sprays. The first one is done for you.

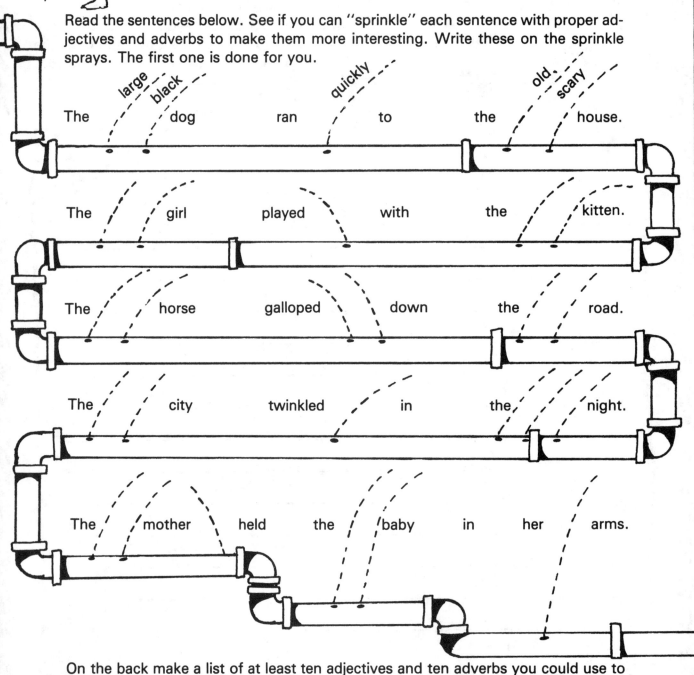

The   large black   dog   ran   quickly   to   the   old scary   house.

The   girl   played   with   the   kitten.

The   horse   galloped   down   the   road.

The   city   twinkled   in   the   night.

The   mother   held   the   baby   in   her   arms.

On the back make a list of at least ten adjectives and ten adverbs you could use to make your sentences better.

24

······ TENNIS TALK! ·····

Bobby Riggs challenged Billie Jean King to a "battle of the sexes." They played that historic match on September 20, 1973. Billie Jean won. She beat Bobby 6-4, 6-3, 6-3.

Read the following terms that relate to tennis below. Circle all action words (verbs).

ace	grip	racket
advantage	ground rules	rally
amateur	gallery	referee
alley	"in play"	serve
backhand stroke	linesman	service
base line	lob	score
bounce	love	singles
court	macadam court	slam into the net
deuce	match play	slice the ball
double fault	mixed doubles	spectators
doubles	net ball	the ready position
equipment	officials	tournament
flat serve	overhead smash	visor
forehand	points	volley
game set	professional	

Below draw "tennis people" using tennis rackets and balls. You may want to use some of the "tennis talk" above.

A RECIPE FOR FALL

On September 22nd or 23rd the fall season begins. This new season is called the "Autumnal Equinox" which means equal night and day, twelve hours of night and twelve hours of day. The sun rises directly in the east and sets directly in the west.

Have you ever read a recipe for cooking or baking? The recipe tells the name of the dish or food, the ingredients and finally directions. Imagine you can change summer into fall. List the ingredients you need and the directions. Use the model to help you write your recipe for fall.

Ingredients: Recipe: Summer Goes Fall

_____ pints of cool air that _____

_____ trees of colored leaves for _____

_____ pinches of frost that _____

_____ of darkness to make the days shorter

Directions:

Mix these together and _____

_____

Bake with the changes and beauty of _____

_____

Serves ___ people.

On the back make up another recipe model to fill in. You may want to fill it in or have a friend fill it in.

SEPARATE YOUR FACTS

The first cream separator patent was granted September 25, 1877, to Wilhelm Lefeldt and Carl Lentsch of Schoeningen, Germany. The machine consisted of a heavy electric rotator that forced the heavy milk to the base of the pan, thus separating the milk from the cream.

Look at the sentences below. See if you can separate the facts from opinions. Write your answer, FACT or OPINION, on each line.

1. George Washington was the first President of the United States.

   _____

2. P.E. class is more fun than art class.

   _____

3. Plants are living things on the earth.

   _____

4. George Washington was the best President the United States ever had.

   _____

5. Roses are the prettiest plants.

   _____

6. Fishing is at its best when done in the evening.

   _____

7. Owls are very wise birds.

   _____

8. New York is both the name of a state and a city.

   _____

9. Baseball is more fun than soccer.

   _____

10. Watermelon is tastier than cantaloupe.

   _____

11. The United States is over 100 years old.

   _____

12. Quarter horses make the best pets.

   _____

13. The dinosaur was a very large animal.

   _____

14. Rembrandt was a famous artist who lived long ago.

   _____

15. Doing this work sheet is more fun than recess.

   _____

Write three fact sentences and three opinion sentences about milk or cream on the back.

CHOO! CHOO! ALL ABOARD!

A locomotive is a machine that moves trains on railroad tracks. Early locomotives weighed from three to six tons and could pull only a few light cars.

Locomotives designed to haul passengers or freight are called road locomotives. The first locomotives pulled a passenger train on September 27, 1825.

Have you ever traveled by train? Not too many people travel by train today. Pretend you are taking a trip on a train. List the things you might see, hear, and smell while on your trip. Write them in the train cars below.

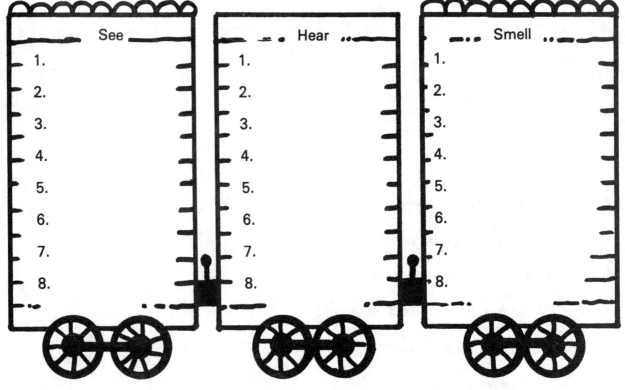

See	Hear	Smell
1.	1.	1.
2.	2.	2.
3.	3.	3.
4.	4.	4.
5.	5.	5.
6.	6.	6.
7.	7.	7.
8.	8.	8.

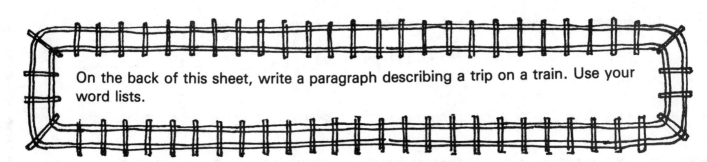

On the back of this sheet, write a paragraph describing a trip on a train. Use your word lists.

TOUCHDOWN!

The first football game to be played at night occurred on September 29, 1892, at Mansfield Fair in Mansfield, Pennsylvania. Twenty electric lights of 2,000 candle power were used to light up the field. The game lasted seventy minutes, but only one half was played.

Read and solve the problems below.

Opponent's side   John's side

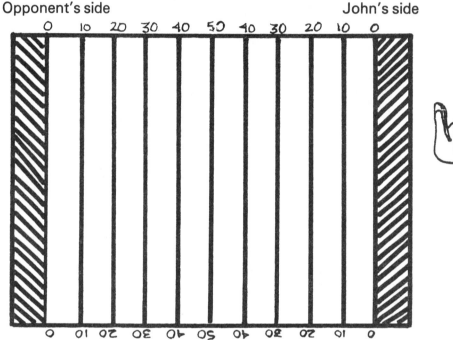

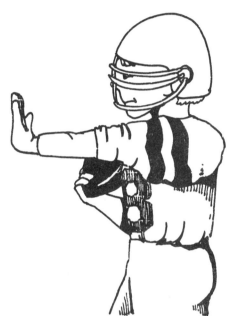

1. John is on the 10-yard line. He runs 15 yards. What yard line is he on now? _____

2. If John's team is on the 25-yard line and they move the ball 5 yards each down, where will they be after their 3rd play? _____

3. John catches the ball on his 30-yard line and runs for 50 yards. How many yards does he have to go to make a touchdown? _____

4. John's team fumbles the ball on his team's 45-yard line. John recovers the ball on his team's 20-yard line. How many yards did John's team lose? _____

5. When John's team makes a touchdown, they receive 6 points. Solve these problems:

   3 touchdowns = _____points

   6 touchdowns = _____points

   5 touchdowns = _____points

SLOCUM'S PIN STICKER

The first stapler was patented on September 30, 1841, by Samuel Slocum of Poughkeepsie, New York. It was called a machine "for sticking pins into paper." A sliding hopper deposited the pins into grooves.

A staple connects two or more articles. Read the two groups below. Rearrange them and "staple" them into pairs to form compound words. Write these new compound words on the lines.

button	corn
pocket	shoe
light	house
waste	board
grand	knife
horse	body
skate	rise
dish	rag
some	hole
sun	fall
pop	basket
water	mother

COMPOUND CONNECTIONS

1. _____
2. _____
3. _____
4. _____
5. _____
6. _____
7. _____
8. _____
9. _____
10. _____
11. _____
12. _____

On the back arrange the compound words in alphabetical order.

WITCHES' BREW

Abra-cadabra, horn of gazelle,
Fly's leg, bat's wing, lizard's tail.
The gills of a fish that smell so weird
Bug's eye, duck's foot, goat's beard.
Heat it up.
Let it boil.
Let it set, ferment and spoil.
Then drink it up quick, it's delicious and rich—
An lo and behold, you're a Halloween witch!

Jocelyn
Age 11

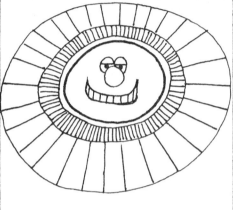

OCTOBER

October

Sunday	Monday	Tuesday	Wednesday	Thursday	Friday	Saturday

A. Run off enough calendars on the opposite page so that each student can have one of his own. You may also want to reproduce the cutouts found at the bottom of this page. The student can use these cutouts as "stickers" for his calendar. If one side of the pattern is put on the fold and the rest is cut out, the student can lift the pattern and write on the inside. These cutout "stickers" can be decorated as the student wishes. The cutout can be taped or glued to the appropriate place on the calendar.

The following activities are suggested uses for the calendar:

1. Each student can write down a "thought for the day" for each day on his calendar. These thoughts can be for a specific topic (ecology, school) or very general. The student can also make a collection of personal and/or published poems. These can be found in libraries. The calendar and written "thoughts" can be the cover for this collection.
2. Have students use the calendar as a cover for health materials and lessons for Children's Health Day. Many pamphlets can be found at your county health department, county extension office and local hospital. Be sure to include the activity found on page 37.

B. Enlarge the calendar (on the opposite page) to design a bulletin board for your classroom. An example is shown above. You may want students to complete ongoing activities to fill in the calendar. One student can be assigned to a specific day of the month. Some suggestions are given below. Enlarge the cutout patterns for students to write down the information they wish to place on the calendar. If one side of the pattern is put on the fold and the rest is cut out, the student can lift the pattern and write on the inside. These cutout "stickers" can be decorated as the student wishes. The cutout can be taped or glued to the appropriate place on the calendar.

1. Have a different student fill in the name of a favorite poem for every day of the month. He can also recite the poem to the class.
2. Have a different student write a health tip for each day of the month. (For example, brush your teeth three times a day; get an annual checkup, etc.)
3. Have a different student write down a use for electricity for each day of the month.

ACTIVITIES FOR OCTOBER

DEAR DIARY

Some famous writers were born in the month of October. Many writers have written books and stories based on their personal notes. Often these notes are just daily happenings from their own lives.

Now is your opportunity to begin the life of a writer. Sometime during each hour today, write about a happening that involves you or of which you are aware.

Date: October _____

9:00 a.m. _____

_____

_____

10:00 a.m. _____

_____

_____

_____

11:00 a.m. _____

_____

_____

_____

12:00 a.m. _____

_____

_____

1:00 p.m. _____

_____

_____

_____

2:00 p.m. _____

_____

_____

_____

Summarize your writing in several paragraphs on the back of this sheet. Also, see if you can find out who some of these famous authors are.

COLOR ME RED

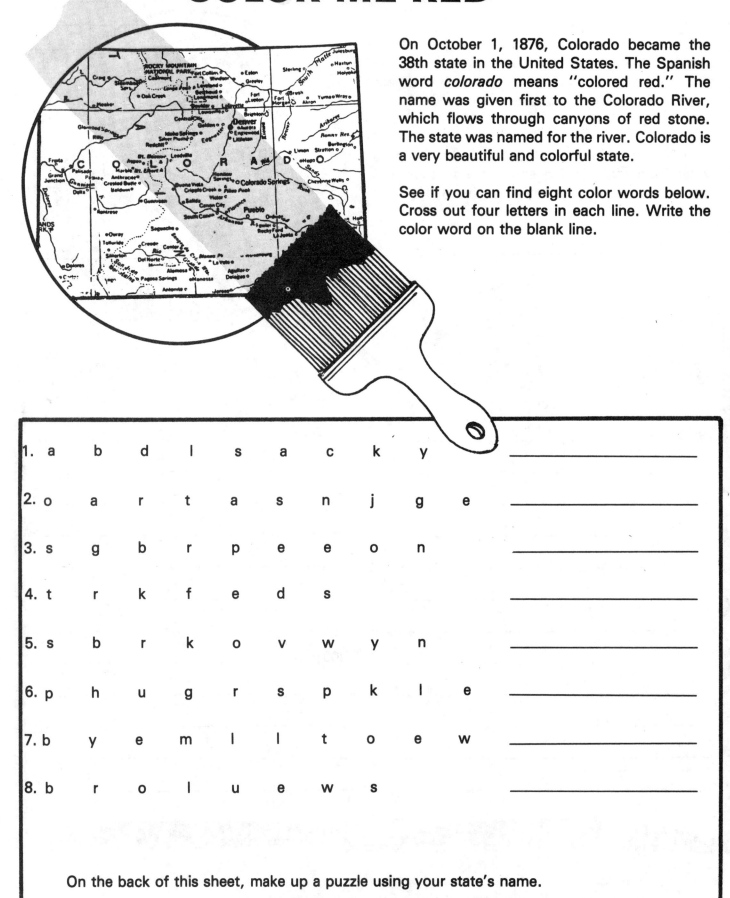

On October 1, 1876, Colorado became the 38th state in the United States. The Spanish word *colorado* means "colored red." The name was given first to the Colorado River, which flows through canyons of red stone. The state was named for the river. Colorado is a very beautiful and colorful state.

See if you can find eight color words below. Cross out four letters in each line. Write the color word on the blank line.

1. a   b   d   l   s   a   c   k   y   _____

2. o   a   r   t   a   s   n   j   g   e   _____

3. s   g   b   r   p   e   e   o   n   _____

4. t   r   k   f   e   d   s   _____

5. s   b   r   k   o   v   w   y   n   _____

6. p   h   u   g   r   s   p   k   l   e   _____

7. b   y   e   m   l   l   t   o   e   w   _____

8. b   r   o   l   u   e   w   s   _____

On the back of this sheet, make up a puzzle using your state's name.

36

TAKE GOOD CARE OF YOURSELF

October 3rd is celebrated as Child Health Day. Good physical health (not being sick or having diseases), good mental health, good nutrition (eating sensibly), safety, and exercise are all necessary in order for a person to be healthy.

Below are questions pertaining to different areas of health. Answer them honestly. Perhaps there is an area you can improve on.

1. Do you know who to call in case of an emergency? _____

2. Who is your doctor? _____

3. Do you know your blood type? _____

4. Are you allergic to anything? If so, what? _____

5. Have you had all your vaccinations? _____

6. What did you have for breakfast today? _____

7. What foods should be included at meals? _____

8. Do you snack between meals? _____

9. What would you do if you saw your little sister or brother swallow some drain cleaner? _____

10. Do you cross streets at crosswalks or in the middle of the street? _____

11. Do you know the "Rules of the Road" for riding your bicycle? _____

12. Do you brush your teeth regularly (2-3 times a day)? _____

On the back draw a picture of a young person your age with good health. Include some of the things mentioned above: good nutrition, safety, exercise, etc.

ITS FIRST BROADCAST

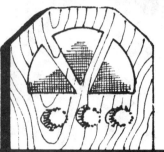

On October 5, 1921, a well-known sporting event was broadcast for the first time. The Giants came face to face with the Yankees.

Decode the words below using the code wheel and try to guess the sporting event that was broadcast before you decode number 10.

1. ___ ___ ___ ___ ___ ___
    19 20 18   9 11   5

2. ___ ___ ___ ___
     2   1 19   5

3. ___ ___ ___ ___
     6 15 21 12

4. ___ ___ ___ ___
     2   1 12 12

5. ___ ___ ___ ___   ___ ___ ___
     8 15 13   5   18 21 14

6. ___ ___ ___ ___ ___ ___
     4 21   7 15 21 20

7. ___ ___ ___ ___ ___ ___ ___
    16   9 20   3   8   5 18

8. ___ ___ ___ ___ ___ ___ ___ ___
    19   8 15 18 20 19 20 15 16

9. ___ ___ ___ ___ ___
     3 15   1   3   8

10. ___ ___ ___ ___ ___   ___ ___ ___ ___ ___ ___
    23 15 18 12   4   19   5 18   9   5 19

On the back of this sheet, write the names of five baseball teams and the cities where they are located. (You may need to use an encyclopedia.)

HICKORY, DICKORY DOCK . . .
A SELF-WINDING CLOCK

The first self-winding clock was made by Benjamin Hanks of Litchfield, Connecticut. He constructed a clock machine that winds itself up by help of the air and will continue to do so without any other aid or assistance. On October 6, 1783, he applied for a 14-year exclusive patent right from the state of Connecticut.

Read the questions below and write your "timely" answers on the lines.

1.   How many months in a year? _____

2.   How many hours in a day? _____

3.   How many days are in a year? _____

4.   How many minutes are in an hour? _____

What are the times shown on the clocks below?

1. _____   2. _____   3. _____   4. _____

   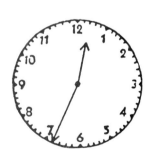

5. _____   6. _____   7. _____   8. _____

On the back make three clocks showing the times 7:42, 11:22, and 12:35.

HOW NOW BROWN COW

The Great Chicago Fire began on October 8, 1871. The week of October 8th is Fire Prevention Week and the anniversary of the fire. Using your encyclopedia, try to find the following information:

1. Who or what started the fire? _____
   _____

2. Where did the fire start? _____
   _____

3. When did the fire start? _____

4. What happened? (How far did it spread? How many people were homeless?) ____
   _____
   _____

5. National Newspaper Week is also in October. It varies from year to year as to the exact time. Using the answers to the above questions, write an article about the Great Chicago Fire.

   _____
   _____
   _____
   _____
   _____
   _____
   _____
   _____
   _____
   _____
   _____

Now write an article describing fire prevention tips that you and your friends can follow. For example, never play with a kerosene heater, especially when it is on. Use the back of this page for your article.

A STRIKE AND A SPARE

The first bowling automatic scorer was used in sanctioned league games on October 10, 1967. The Brunswick Automatic Scorer was installed in a 16-lane bowling center in Chicago. It automatically recorded pinfall, ball by ball, frame by frame; computed and totaled individual and team scores; and in a fraction of a second, printed scores on a permanent scorecard and projected them onto an easy-to-view overhead screen.

Look at the bowling scorecard below. Use this information to answer the questions given to you.

PLAYER	1	2	3	4	5	6	7	8	9	10	TOTAL
	6 3	8 /	5 2	X	8 1	4 3	9 /	5 4	X	X 7 2	
Tim	9	24	31	50	59	66	81	90	117	136	136

PLAYER	1	2	3	4	5	6	7	8	9	10	TOTAL
	X	X	X	X	X	X	X	X	X	X X X	
Joan	30	60	90	120	150	180	210	240	270	300	300

PLAYER	1	2	3	4	5	6	7	8	9	10	TOTAL
	9 /	9 /	9 /	9 /	9 /	9 /	9 /	9 /	9 /	9 / 9	
Ken	19	38	57	76	95	114	133	152	171	190	190

PLAYER	1	2	3	4	5	6	7	8	9	10	TOTAL
	5 4	7 /	X	5 4	4 2	8 /	5 3	6 /	5 4	6 / 5	
Bill	9	29	48	57	63	78	86	101	110	125	125

1. Which player had the highest score at the end of the game? _____

2. What was the total score of all four players in frame 4? _____

3. What was the total score for all four players in frame 8? _____

4. Which player had the lowest score at the end of the game? _____

5. Which player had the lowest score in frame 7? _____

6. How many points more did Joan have at the end of the game than Bill? _____

7. How many points more did Ken have than Tim at the end of the game? _____

8. What was the total score for all four players at the end of the game? _____

9. On the back compute how much better Joan did than Tim on *each* frame. List your answers.

41

ABSOLUTELY ACCURATE

On October 11, 1887, the patent for the first adding machine, absolutely accurate at all times, was issued. This machine was named the Comptometer. It was invented by Dorr Eugene Felt of Chicago, Illinois.

Solve the problem below. Arrange the numerals 0, 1, 2, 3, 4, 5, 6, 7, 8, 9 in the boxes below to make a true equation. You may use each numeral *only once.* Record at least ten solutions on the lines below.

$$\begin{array}{r} \square\,\square\,,\,\square\,\square\,\square \\ +\ \square\,\square\,,\,\square\,\square\,\square \\ \hline \mathbf{9\,9\,,\,9\,9\,9} \end{array}$$

1. _____   6. _____

2. _____   7. _____

3. _____   8. _____

4. _____   9. _____

5. _____   10. _____

Write each solution you did on the back of this sheet. Then, subtract ninety-nine from each set of numerals. Have a friend check your problems to see if you are as accurate as an absolutely accurate adding machine!

A NICE BIRTHDAY PRESENT

The first President's wife to be depicted on a commemorative postage stamp was Anna Eleanor Roosevelt (Mrs. Franklin Delano Roosevelt). On October 11, 1963, her picture appeared on the 5-cent light purple stamp issued at Washington, D.C., on the anniversary of her birthday.

Design a stamp honoring a special person or place in the space given below.

Write an explanation of your stamp design on the lines below. Your paragraph should answer *who, when, where* and *why* about your stamp person or place.

_____

_____

_____

_____

_____

_____

_____

_____

Look up Anna Eleanor Roosevelt in the encyclopedia and write two interesting facts about her on the back of this sheet.

LOOK INTO THE FUTURE

On October 12, 1492, Christopher Columbus discovered North America. He thought he had sailed around the world and landed at India. Therefore he called the native people "Indians." If Columbus could have looked into the future, he would have never imagined the world as it is today: television, telephone, computers, video games, etc.

Look into the future and see what the future, the next 500 years, has to offer. Choose one of the subjects from below and *draw* it or *write* about it in the space provided. If you wish to do more, use the back of this page.

School	Sports and Recreation	Telephones
Spaceships	Jobs	Medicines
Land Transportation	Food and Drinks	Toys
Energy Systems	Clothing	Crafts
Television	Homes and Furniture	Tools
Illnesses	Books and Magazines	Supermarkets

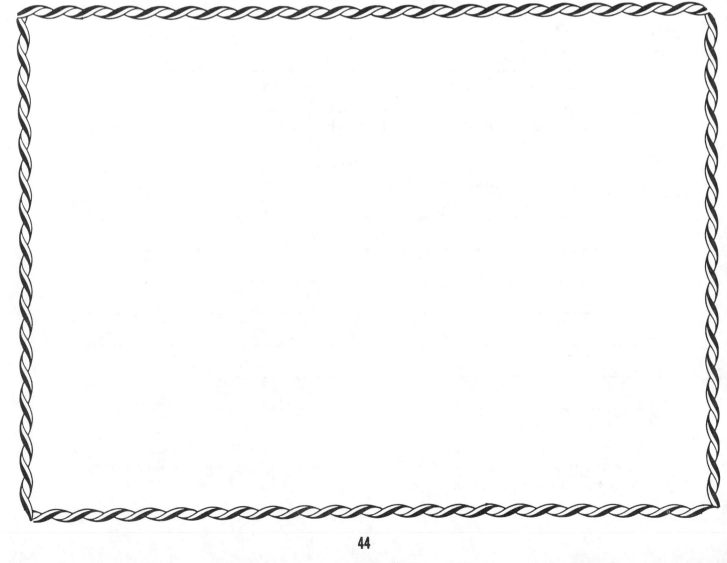

DID YOU HEAR THAT?

How fast is the speed of sound? A plane reaching the speed of sound is said to be breaking the sound or sonic barrier. The first person to break the sound barrier was Captain Charles E. Yeager of the U.S. Air Force. He did this in a Bell X-1 rocket plane on October 14, 1947.

Solve the problems below. The answer to number 5 is the number of miles per hour sound travels (speed of sound).

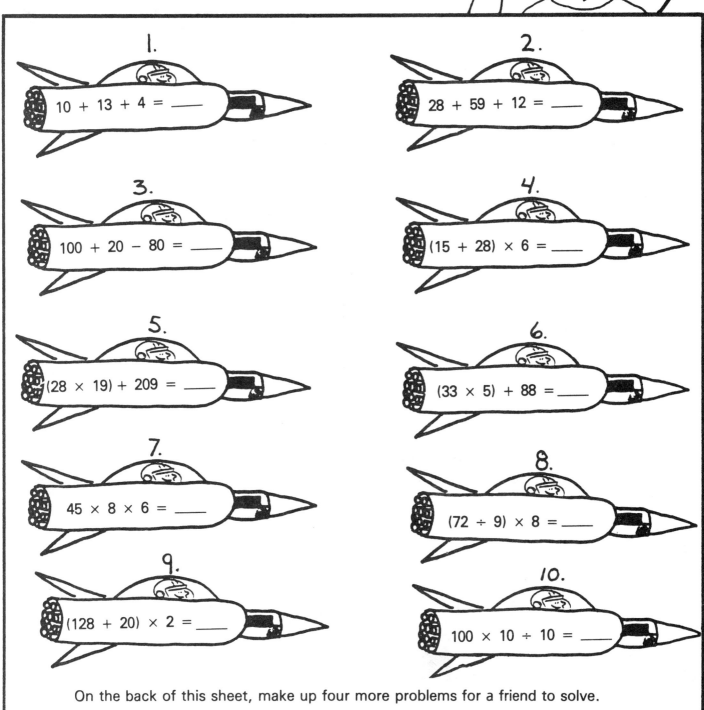

1. $10 + 13 + 4 =$ _____

2. $28 + 59 + 12 =$ _____

3. $100 + 20 - 80 =$ _____

4. $(15 + 28) \times 6 =$ _____

5. $(28 \times 19) + 209 =$ _____

6. $(33 \times 5) + 88 =$ _____

7. $45 \times 8 \times 6 =$ _____

8. $(72 \div 9) \times 8 =$ _____

9. $(128 + 20) \times 2 =$ _____

10. $100 \times 10 \div 10 =$ _____

On the back of this sheet, make up four more problems for a friend to solve.

ARE YOU A POET, AND DON'T KNOW IT?

Besides being famous for authors, October is also famous for poets. On October 14, 1894, e.e. cummings was born. October 15 is designated as National Poetry Day. Finally, Jupiter Hammon, the first black American to publish his poetry, was born on October 17, 1711. In honor of his birthday, that day is designated Black Poetry Day.

The following are two Halloween poems:

PUMPKIN VILLAGE!

On Halloween I ate so much pumpkin pie
My tummy ached so that I was sure I'd die.
Went to sleep—had a nightmare.
Saw a village with pumpkins everywhere.

Hallowy Hallowy Ween!
Time of many a scary scene.
Be distracted, use your wit
By doing these lessons bit by bit.

Find a poem written by e.e. cummings. Print it here.

Find a poem written by Jupiter Hammon. Print it here.

Make your own poem. It could be a haiku or limerick. Print it here. Illustrate it if you wish. You may have to use the back.

LET'S GO TO SKI SCHOOL

Can you snow ski? Many people enjoy learning to ski in the many ski areas throughout the United States. Some people even learn the art of skiing indoors. The first indoor ski school was open October 16, 1939, in Boston, Massachusetts.

Ski the downhill course. Solve problem 1. Use this answer in the blank of problem 2. Your answer for 2 will be the number you put in problem 3. Continue this to problem 7. If your last answer is ninety-nine, you made it.

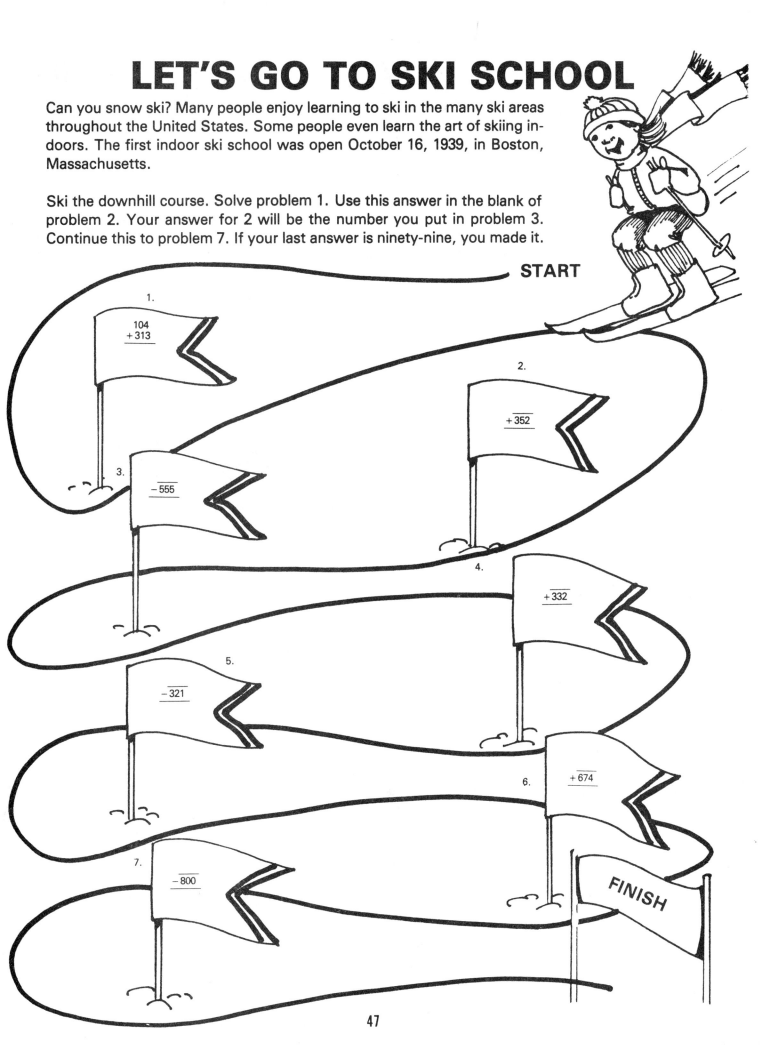

START

1.
```
  104
+ 313
```

2.
```
+ 352
```

3.
```
- 555
```

4.
```
+ 332
```

5.
```
- 321
```

6.
```
+ 674
```

7.
```
- 800
```

FINISH

47

REACH OUT, REACH OUT . . . AND JUST SAY "HI!"

Long distance dial telephone service began October 17, 1949. Mark Sullivan, president of the Pacific Telephone Company in New York City, dialed Oakland, California, and spoke to the president of the Bell Telephone Laboratories, Dr. Oliver E. Buckley. The call was completed in less than one minute.

A person can save money on long distance phone calls by dialing direct and by calling on weekends or at night.

Read the chart below and compute the amount you would pay for each direct dial call. Write your answer on the line next to each problem.

DIRECT DIAL RATES

Additional savings apply evenings, nights and weekends.

	M	T	W	T	F	S	S
8 a.m. to 5 p.m.	■	■	■	■	■	□	□
5 p.m. to 11 p.m.	▨	▨	▨	▨	▨	□	▨
11 p.m. to 8 a.m.	□	□	□	□	□	□	□

Dial-direct	Weekday full rate ■		Evening 35% discount ▨		Night & weekend 60% discount □	
Sample rates from city of Phoenix to	First minute	Each additional minute	First minute	Each additional minute	First minute	Each additional minute
Birmingham, AL	.64	.44	.41	.29	.25	.18
Boise, ID	.61	.42	.39	.28	.24	.17
Chicago, IL	.64	.44	.41	.29	.25	.18
Denver, CO	.61	.42	.39	.28	.24	.17
El Paso, TX	.58	.42	.37	.28	.23.	.17
Hartford, CT	.66	.46	.42	.30	.26	.19
Los Angeles, CA	.58	.42	.37	.28	.23	.17
Miami, FL	.66	.46	.42	.30	.26	.19
New York, NY	.66	.46	.42	.30	.26	.19
Portland, OR	.64	.44	.41	.29	.25	.18
San Francisco, CA	.61	.42	.39	.28	.24	.17
Seattle, WA	.64	.44	.41	.29	.25	.18

1. A 4-minute call from Phoenix to Chicago on a Wednesday at 3:00 p.m.

   cost _____

2. A 20-minute call from Phoenix to Los Angeles on Saturday evening at 10:00 p.m.

   cost _____

3. A 17-minute call from Phoenix to New York on Sunday at 7:00 p.m.

   cost _____

4. A 5-minute call from Phoenix to Boise on Monday morning at 8:30 a.m.

   cost _____

5. A 30-minute call from Phoenix to El Paso on Thursday evening at 11:30 p.m.

   cost _____

On the back of this sheet, make up four telephone problems and share them with a friend.

OUR FAMOUS LADY

The Statue of Liberty was a gift from France to the United States. On October 18, 1886, the Statue of Liberty was dedicated by President Grover Cleveland. The statue was unveiled before representatives from France and the United States. On a tablet in the pedestal is a poem. It reads:

Not like the *brazen* giant of Greek fame,
   With conquering limbs *astride* from land to land
   Here at our sea-washed, sunset gates shall stand
A mighty woman with a torch, whose flame
Is the *imprisoned* lightning, and her name
   Mother of Exiles. From her *beacon*-hand
   Glows world-wide welcome; her mild eyes *command*
The air-bridged harbor that twin cities frame.
"Keep *ancient* lands, your storied pomp!" cried she
   With silent lips. "Give me your tired, your poor,
Your huddled masses *yearning* to breathe free,
   The wretched refuse of your teeming shore.
Send these, the homeless, tempest-tost to me,
   I lift my lamp beside the golden door!"

Below are definitions of the italicized words found in the poem. Write the correct word next to the correct definition.

1. _____ made of brass: sounding harsh and loud like struck brass.

2. _____ a signal for guidance

3. _____ to have authority and control over: to direct authoritatively

4. _____ having existed for many years

5. _____ to feel a longing or craving

6. _____ with one leg on each side

7. _____ to put in or as if in prison: confine

 On the back of this sheet, write what the occasion was that prompted France to give the United States the Statue of Liberty.

WHAT A SHOCK!

Benjamin Franklin was one of the first men to experiment with electricity. On October 19, 1752, he flew a home-made kite during a thunderstorm. A bolt of lightning struck the kite and traveled down to a key at the end of the kite. There was a spark, which proved that lightning is electricity.

Find ten words that were used in the story and circle them in the puzzle below.

p	o	t	n	k	e	y	z	t	u	a	b
f	r	a	n	k	l	i	n	k	b	d	f
l	e	o	t	a	e	h	j	m	o	q	s
u	w	y	a	c	c	d	f	b	o	l	t
h	j	l	n	g	t	o	t	e	v	i	x
b	d	f	h	e	r	c	f	n	t	g	f
w	m	s	t	k	i	t	e	j	o	h	x
c	e	f	g	m	c	o	o	a	b	t	d
s	p	a	r	k	i	b	d	m	e	n	g
w	v	t	x	x	t	e	n	i	r	i	o
y	e	f	m	q	y	r	p	n	r	n	b
e	x	p	e	r	i	m	e	n	t	g	x

On the back of this sheet, put the ten words you circled in alphabetical order.

OLD IRONSIDES

The battleship *Constitution* was launched on October 21, 1797. It was built at a Boston shipyard between 1794 and 1797. It was 204 feet long. The hull was made of oak, and the masts were made of white pine. In battle, the ship earned the name "Old Ironsides," because it was said that cannonballs bounced off her sides.

Measure the distance of each cannonball and write that distance on the line. (¼ inch = 10 feet)

1. __80 ft.__

2. _____

3. _____

4. _____

5. _____

6. _____

7. _____

The total distance traveled by all of the cannonballs: _____

51

"ROLL OUT THE BARREL"

The first person to go over Niagara Falls in a barrel was Anna Edson Taylor. On October 24, 1901, she went over the Horseshoe Falls on the Canadian side in a barrel 4½ feet high and 3 feet in diameter.

Think of six words which would describe how you would feel if you were inside a barrel going over Niagara Falls. Write them on the lines below.

_____

_____

Write six words which describe sounds you would hear if you were in a barrel going over the Falls.

_____

_____

Write the meanings of the sentences below.
a.   "The man was as round as a barrel."

_____

_____

b.   "I found myself looking down the barrel of his gun."

_____

_____

Write a short paragraph describing an adventure during which you tumble over Niagara Falls in a barrel.

_____

_____

_____

_____

_____

_____

_____

"LET THERE BE PEACE ON EARTH"

October 24 is United Nations Day in honor of the 1945 adoption of the U.N. Charter. Fifty-one nations signed the Charter at the meeting organized in San Francisco. More nations have joined since then. The United Nations has an area of land and several buildings in New York City. Much business takes place there every day. The purpose of the U.N. is to help keep world peace. The U.N. also helps underdeveloped nations in many areas.

It is a hard job to keep people living together in peace. Different countries speak different languages, have different customs, religions, and life-styles. Choose one of the original fifty-one countries in the United Nations and find out about its customs, life-styles, weather and climate, schooling, etc. Write your report on the lines below.

Argentina	Czechoslovakia	Haiti	New Zealand	Turkey
Australia	Denmark	Honduras	Nicaragua	Ukrainian S.S.R.
Belgium	Dominican Republic	India	Norway	Union of South Africa
Bolivia	Equador	Iran	Panama	USSR
Brazil	Egypt	Iraq	Paraguay	United Kingdom
Byelorussian S.S.R.	El Salvador	Lebanon	Peru	United States
Canada	Ethiopia	Liberia	Philippines	Uruguay
Chile	France	Luxembourg	Poland	Venezuela
China	Greece	Mexico	Saudi Arabia	Yugoslavia
Colombia	Guatemala	Netherlands	Syria	
Costa Rica				
Cuba				

"CLINTON'S DITCH"

The Erie Canal opened on October 26, 1825. Many people made fun of it and called it "Clinton's Ditch" after Governor of New York, DeWitt Clinton. The canal, 350 miles long, links Lake Erie (Buffalo) with the Hudson River (Albany). Despite the initial criticism, the canal became a very busy place. Later, it was widened and deepened and became a part of the New York State Barge Canal.

1. What other canals can you think of? List them here.

    _____

    _____

    _____

2. What are the two canals that are over 700 years old but still in use (or parts are in use)?

    _____

    _____

Below is a map of some of the most famous canals in the world. Put the correct names in the blanks below the map.

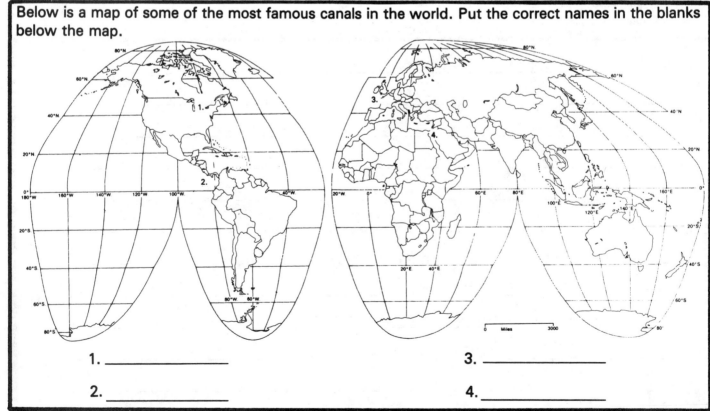

1. _____   3. _____

2. _____   4. _____

SUB POWER

The New York Subway opened on October 27, 1904. On October 28, 1957, the first nuclear-powered submarine, the *Nautilus*, returned to Groton, Connecticut, after being submerged for two weeks in the North Atlantic Ocean. The *Nautilus* broke all previous records for underwater speed and endurance.

Submerse yourself in vocabulary words! You will find the prefix *sub* in each word below. Read each word and each meaning given. Write the correct word on the line next to its meaning.

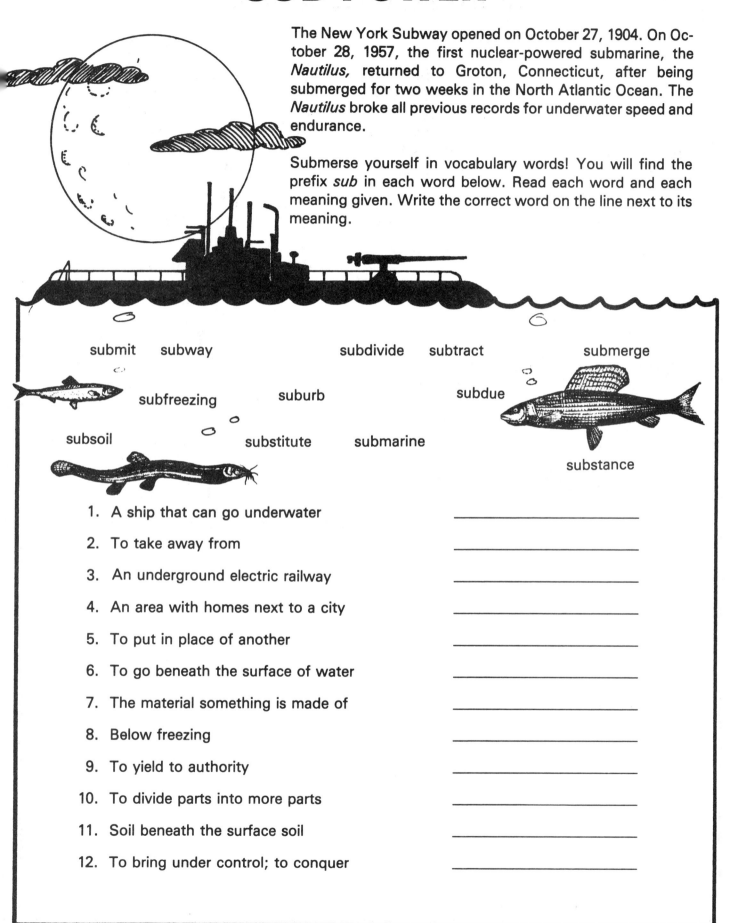

submit   subway   subdivide   subtract   submerge

         subfreezing   suburb   subdue

subsoil   substitute   submarine

                                             substance

1. A ship that can go underwater   _____

2. To take away from   _____

3. An underground electric railway   _____

4. An area with homes next to a city   _____

5. To put in place of another   _____

6. To go beneath the surface of water   _____

7. The material something is made of   _____

8. Below freezing   _____

9. To yield to authority   _____

10. To divide parts into more parts   _____

11. Soil beneath the surface soil   _____

12. To bring under control; to conquer   _____

FINGERPRINTS TALK!

On October 28, 1904, the St. Louis Metropolitan Police Department adopted the fingerprinting system to aid in law enforcement. John M. Shea was the first to qualify as a fingerprint expert connected with any police service. The St. Louis Metropolitan Police Department hired him to fingerprint persons arrested on serious charges.

Look at the fingerprint pictures below. Decide what conversation is being stated in each box and write it on the line next to each picture. Don't forget to use quotation marks and other proper punctuation.

In the empty box below, draw your own fingerprint picture and conversation. You may want to share it with a friend.

PROJECT CIRRUS

The first forest fire drenched by artificial rain took place on October 29, 1947, at Concord, New Hampshire. The artificial rain was produced by seeding cumulus clouds with dry ice. "Rainmaking" planes flew over the burning area and caused rain to fall. The experiment was called PROJECT CIRRUS.

Read the list of words below. They are all found in a forest. Then, write each word under the correct heading of PLANT, ANIMAL, or EARTH.

mountain	moose	hare	fern	ivy
squirrel	gully	fox	buck	logs
buttercup	grasses	doe	ditch	moss
bush	trees	bear	valley	
raccoon				

	PLANT	ANIMAL	EARTH
1.	bush		
2.			
3.			
4.			
5.			
6.			
7.			
8.			

On the back make a list of ten other things you could see in a forest. Put them in alphabetical order.

THE CARD TIME RECORDER

Many people who work record the days and number of hours worked each day. The recording is done automatically on a Card Time Recorder. The first Card Time Recorder was invented by Daniel M. Cooper of Rochester, New York, on October 30, 1887.

Read and solve the questions below, by looking at James's and Larry's time cards. Note: James and Larry are paid $5.00 per hour.

James

DATE	IN	OUT	TOTAL HOURS
Mon.	8:00	5:00	9
Tues.	9:30	3:30	6
Wed.	8:00	4:00	8
Thurs.	7:00	3:00	8
Fri.	8:00	4:30	8 ½

Larry

DATE	IN	OUT	TOTAL HOURS
Mon.	8:00	4:00	8
Tues.	9:30	3:30	6
Wed.	8:00	4:30	8 ½
Thurs.	8:30	4:00	7 ½
Fri.	9:00	4:00	7

1. What is the total number of hours worked by James? _____

2. How much money will James earn for his five days work? _____

3. How much money will Larry earn for Monday, Tuesday and Wednesday? _____

   _____

4. Who earns the most money for five days work? _____

5. If James had worked until 5:00 o'clock on Wednesday, how much money would he have earned that day? _____

6. If Larry is paid every two weeks, what will be his total amount of money earned ? _____

7. If Larry works an additional hour each day, how much will he earn for one week's work? _____

8. What is the total amount of money earned by both James and Larry for one week's work? _____

58

THE BATTLE-BORN STATE

On October 31, 1864, Nevada became the 36th state. The capital of Nevada is Carson City. Nevada comes from the Spanish word meaning "snow-clad." Nevada has the nickname of the Silver State because of large amounts of silver once mined in the area. Sometimes Nevada is called the Battle-Born State because it became a state during the Civil War.

Read the questions and answer each question by checking the yes or no box.

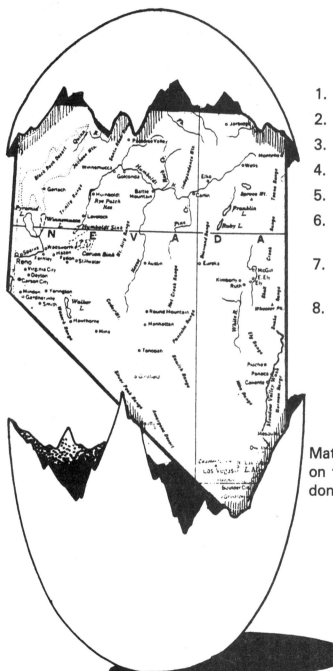

1. Nevada is the 37th state.
2. Nevada is a Spanish word.
3. The capital is Carson City.
4. Nevada means "snow-clad."
5. The state has three nicknames.
6. Nevada is called the Battle-Born State.
7. Nevada became a state on October 30th.
8. Silver was once mined in Nevada.

Yes	No
w	✓ v
a	c
e	n
l	o
i	s
a	j
r	g
s	m

Match the letters in the boxes you checked and write them on the correct problem numbers below. The first one is done for you.

A well-known city in Nevada

___ ___ ___ V ___ ___ ___ ___
 4   6   5   1   3   7   2   8

On the back of this sheet, make five words using the letters from the word *Nevada.* You can use the letters more than once.

THE MAGIC E!

October 31 is designated National Magic Day. A famous person, Harry Houdini, died in 1926 on this day.

The letter "e" has magic in it. Add an "e" to each of the following words and put the new word in the blank. Then answer the questions with either the original word or the new word you made. The first one is done for you.

1. plum + e = ___plume___   Which word is the feather? ___plume___

2. twin + e = _____   Which word is a person? _____

3. cod + e = _____   Which word is a fish? _____

4. spin + e = _____   Which word is a part of the body? _____

5. slim + e = _____   Which word means thin? _____

6. mar + e = _____   Which word could gallop? _____

7. cub + e = _____   Which word is a baby bear? _____

8. gal + e = _____   Which word is a female? _____

9. glob + e = _____   Which word is round? _____

10. scar + e = _____   Which word is a Halloween word? _____

11. Add a few samples of your own in the space below.

_____   _____

_____   _____

_____   _____

Illustrate one of the magic "e" words or one that you made up.

NOVEMBER

Be different
Go your own way.
Do what you think is right.
Look back at yourself
   at the end of the day.
Do you like what you see?
What did you learn?
   What did you find?
Where did you make the mistake?

Stephanie
Age 11

NOVEMBER

November

Sunday	Monday	Tuesday	Wednesday	Thursday	Friday	Saturday

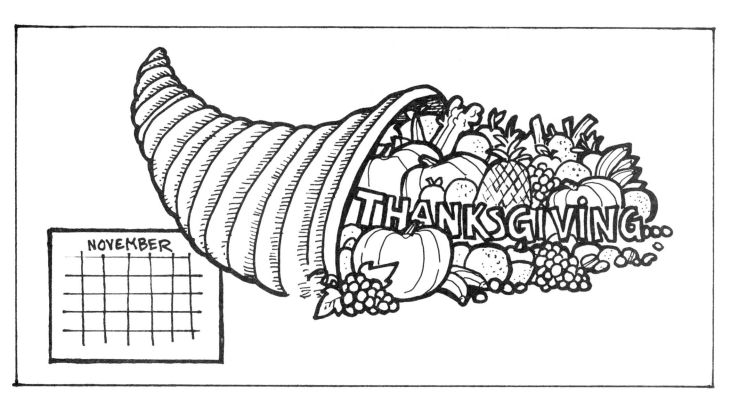

A. Run off enough calendars on the opposite page so that each student can have one of his own. You may also want to reproduce the cutouts found at the bottom of this page. The student can use these cutouts as "stickers" for his calendar. If one side of the pattern is put on the fold and the rest is cut out, the student can lift the pattern and write on the inside. These cutout "stickers" can be decorated as the student wishes. The cutout can be taped or glued to the appropriate place on the calendar.

The following activities are suggested uses for the calendar:

1. Each student can do a cat booklet of the history, breeds and life facts about cats. *The World Book Encyclopedia* or any "cat" book would be a good reference. The calendar can be included in the booklet with cutouts on the days the student found a new fact about cats.
2. Each student could collect materials (information, articles of clothing, pottery, etc.) about Indians. These could be used in class discussion or a show 'n tell. With his calendar, he can make a calendar countdown (by marking off the days) until Indian Heritage Day (November 25).
3. National Stamp Collector's Week is in November. Each student can put a cutout on his calendar on each day he added an item to one of his own collections (stamp, airplane, etc.) or started a new collection.

B. Enlarge the calendar (on the opposite page) to design a bulletin board for your classroom. An example is shown above. You may want students to complete ongoing activities to fill in the calendar. One student can be assigned to a specific day of the month. Some suggestions are given below. Enlarge the cutout patterns for students to write down the information they wish to place on the calendar. If one side of the pattern is put on the fold and the rest is cut out, the student can lift the pattern and write on the inside. These cutout "stickers" can be decorated as the student wishes. The cutout can be taped or glued to the appropriate place on the calendar.

1. Have a different student write down something to be thankful for each day.
2. Have a different student write down the name of a breed of cat for each day. No breed should appear twice.
3. Have a different student write down the name of an Indian tribe for each day. Also have the student name a unique trait about each tribe. Try to avoid repetition as much as possible.

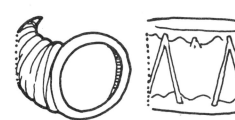   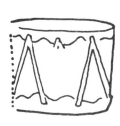

ACTIVITIES FOR NOVEMBER

CATS FOR ALL SEASONS

The week beginning with the first Sunday in November is designated as National Cat Week. Many different "cats" are listed below. See if you can match the right definition with the right "cat."

a. _____ catgut

b. _____ catapult

c. _____ caterwaul

d. _____ catacombs

e. _____ catsup

f. _____ catalogue

g. _____ catnip

h. _____ cataract

i. _____ cathead

j. _____ cattail

k. _____ catkin

l. _____ catfish

m. _____ catbird

n. _____ caterpillar

o. _____ catastrophe

p. _____ catwalk

1. the cry of an angry tomcat

2. a red and spicy cat

3. can be found in wet marshes in the fall of the year

4. belongs to the mint family

5. a list of items usually in alphabetical order

6. used in making strings for a violin

7. has wings and flies

8. a sudden disaster

9. swims in water and is used as a food

10. a narrow bridge or pathway

11. eventually grows beautiful wings

12. a large waterfall

13. always underground

14. used for throwing rocks and stones

15. part of a sailing ship

16. can be found on the branches of a willow tree in springtime

Pick one of the "cats" above and illustrate it in the box below.

A CHANGE IN THE WEATHER

November 1, 1870, was the date that the U.S. Weather Bureau made their first weather observation. Many people had folkways of forecasting the weather. Below is a list of ways to forecast weather. Classify them **F** for folk; **M** for modern.

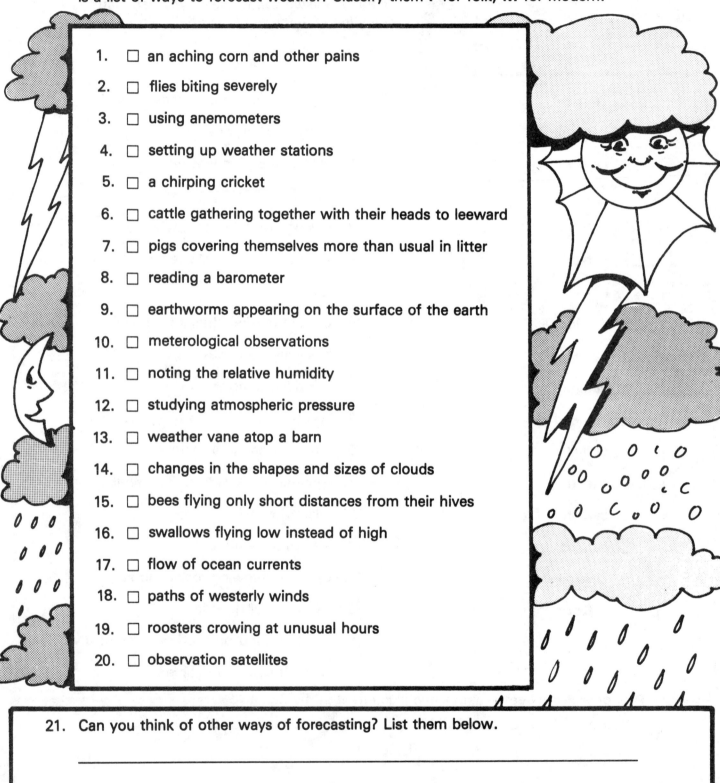

1. ☐ an aching corn and other pains
2. ☐ flies biting severely
3. ☐ using anemometers
4. ☐ setting up weather stations
5. ☐ a chirping cricket
6. ☐ cattle gathering together with their heads to leeward
7. ☐ pigs covering themselves more than usual in litter
8. ☐ reading a barometer
9. ☐ earthworms appearing on the surface of the earth
10. ☐ meterological observations
11. ☐ noting the relative humidity
12. ☐ studying atmospheric pressure
13. ☐ weather vane atop a barn
14. ☐ changes in the shapes and sizes of clouds
15. ☐ bees flying only short distances from their hives
16. ☐ swallows flying low instead of high
17. ☐ flow of ocean currents
18. ☐ paths of westerly winds
19. ☐ roosters crowing at unusual hours
20. ☐ observation satellites

21. Can you think of other ways of forecasting? List them below.

_____

_____

On the back research one of the ways listed above.

A FAMOUS PIONEER

Born November 2, 1734, this famous pioneer of colonial times explored the unknown forests and meadows of Kentucky. He was a natural leader and, in times of trouble, people turned to him for help.

Like most pioneer children, he had little chance to go to school. He did learn to read, write, and use numbers, but his spelling was poor. This man knew how to survive in the wilderness surrounded by fierce animals. Today he is pictured as the ideal frontiersman.

To find out who this man was, first solve the problems. Next, match the products with the letters above the problems. Write the letter on the line above the correct product. The first one is done for you.

B	D	E	O	E
362	574	281	693	438
×8	×7	×8	×7	×4
2896				

O	N	L	I	A	N
63	49	87	35	97	411
×7	×6	×6	×8	×8	×7

                                                  B

___	___	___	___	___	___		___	___	___	___	___
4018	776	294	280	2248	522		2896	4851	441	2877	1752

On the back of this sheet, make up five more problems for a friend to solve.

A SANDWICH IS A SANDWICH

On November 3, 1718, the inventor of the sandwich, John Montagu, the fourth Earl of Sandwich, was born. The story goes that he was a gambler who found that putting meat between slices of bread allowed him to eat without interrupting his gambling.

Choose your favorite sandwich. Explain in writing how to make your sandwich. Use these words to help you in your writing: *first, next, then, don't forget, remember* and *finally.*

WAGON TRAIN, OOH!

On November 4, 1841, the first immigrant wagon train arrived in California. These settlers were led by John Bidwell, a schoolteacher, and John Bartleson, a wagon master and land speculator. They drove their long wagon train through the mountain passes to make their home in this new Mexican territory which is now called California.

See if you can turn your mind towards vocabulary words and fill in the wagon wheels with words fitting the same category. Write the category on the line under each wheel. The first one is done for you.

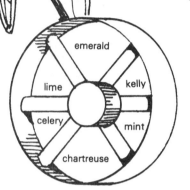

1. shades of green

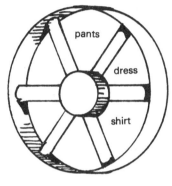

2. _____

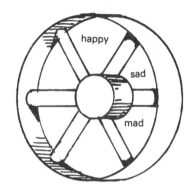

3. _____

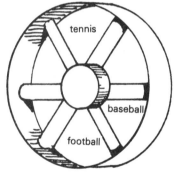

4. _____

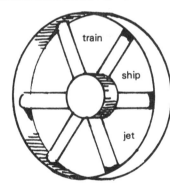

5. _____

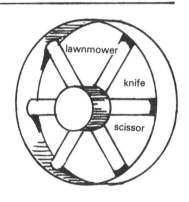

6. _____

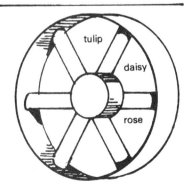

7. _____

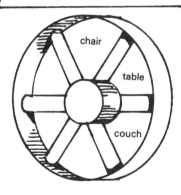

8. _____

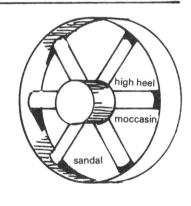

9. _____

On the back make five wheel category problems of your own and have a friend fill them in.

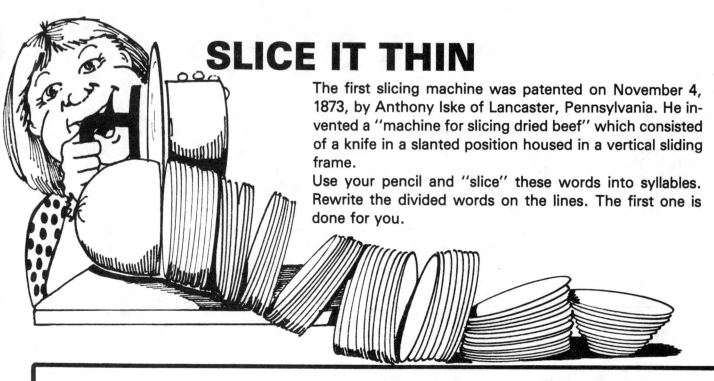

SLICE IT THIN

The first slicing machine was patented on November 4, 1873, by Anthony Iske of Lancaster, Pennsylvania. He invented a "machine for slicing dried beef" which consisted of a knife in a slanted position housed in a vertical sliding frame.

Use your pencil and "slice" these words into syllables. Rewrite the divided words on the lines. The first one is done for you.

1. rib/bon _____rib/bon_____

2. seldom _____

3. final _____

4. tablet _____

5. gossip _____

6. vibrate _____

7. rumor _____

8. message _____

9. whisper _____

10. hotel _____

11. suddenly _____

12. absolute _____

13. volcano _____

14. splendid _____

15. suffer _____

16. calculate _____

17. muffin _____

18. equator _____

19. republic _____

20. ballot _____

Choose five words from above and use each in a sentence on the back.

HOW DO WE GET THERE?

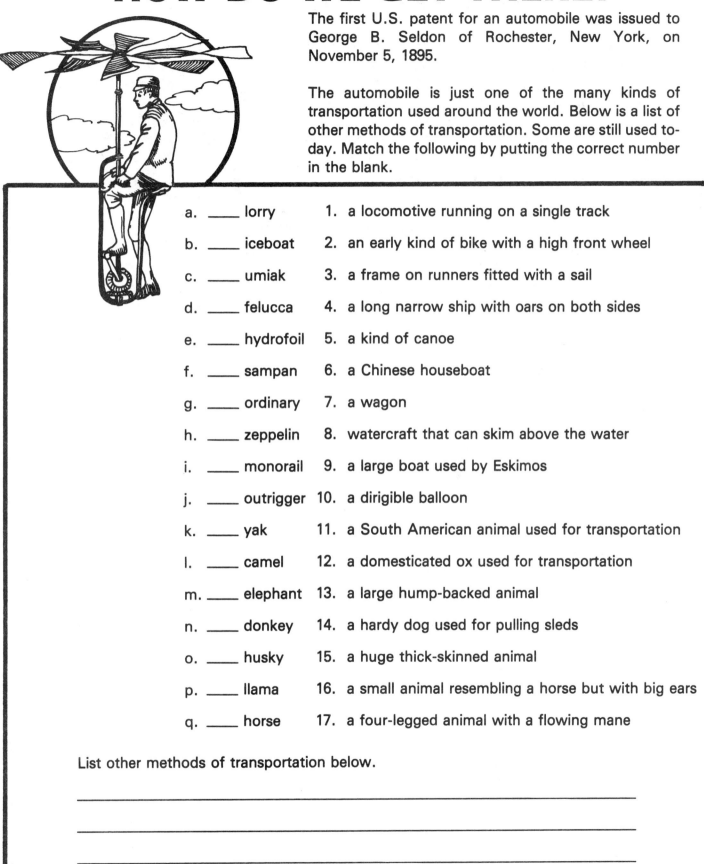

The first U.S. patent for an automobile was issued to George B. Seldon of Rochester, New York, on November 5, 1895.

The automobile is just one of the many kinds of transportation used around the world. Below is a list of other methods of transportation. Some are still used today. Match the following by putting the correct number in the blank.

a. ____ lorry

b. ____ iceboat

c. ____ umiak

d. ____ felucca

e. ____ hydrofoil

f. ____ sampan

g. ____ ordinary

h. ____ zeppelin

i. ____ monorail

j. ____ outrigger

k. ____ yak

l. ____ camel

m. ____ elephant

n. ____ donkey

o. ____ husky

p. ____ llama

q. ____ horse

1. a locomotive running on a single track

2. an early kind of bike with a high front wheel

3. a frame on runners fitted with a sail

4. a long narrow ship with oars on both sides

5. a kind of canoe

6. a Chinese houseboat

7. a wagon

8. watercraft that can skim above the water

9. a large boat used by Eskimos

10. a dirigible balloon

11. a South American animal used for transportation

12. a domesticated ox used for transportation

13. a large hump-backed animal

14. a hardy dog used for pulling sleds

15. a huge thick-skinned animal

16. a small animal resembling a horse but with big ears

17. a four-legged animal with a flowing mane

List other methods of transportation below.

_____

_____

_____

Draw your favorite form of transportation on the back.

STATEHOOD

Four states were admitted to the Union in November of the same year. Two states, North Dakota and South Dakota, were admitted on the same day, November 2, as the 39th and 40th states. President Cleveland signed the Admission Act and President Harrison signed the Proclamations of Admission. Montana was admitted November 8 as the 41st state and Washington was admitted on November 11 as the 42nd state.

Read the puzzle below. Color in all words having a prefix or suffix. Look carefully and it will tell you the year in which these four states joined the Union.

North Dakota, South Dakota, Washington and Montana were admitted in....

	pelt			cream	wrath			blunt			
collection		sweetly				illness			unfit	disown	exchange
blackness	uncut	speck	exclaim	enlist	dodge	exclaim	discolor	flight	unreal		
express	unwise	stray	disarm	undue	speck	unpack	laughable	truthful	unfair		
unfold	swept	payable	cloak	plump	enrich	grasp	wring	speech	skillful		
dislike	joyous	balm	helpful	compound	weld	express	stain	crept	richness		
restful	handful	bulb	untold	disband	fleet	uneasy	notch	stalk	painful		
unripe	wept	sadness	scalp	least	disable	state	castle	knack	darkness		

Look up the capitals of these four states.

1. The capital of North Dakota is _____.

2. The capital of South Dakota is _____.

3. The capital of Montana is _____.

4. The capital of Washington is _____.

BLACK IS BEAUTIFUL

The first blackout for New York City, New England and Canada occurred on November 9, 1965.

Below is a list of "black" words. Match them with their meanings.

a. ____ black birds

b. ____ black gum

c. ____ blackball

d. ____ "black and blue"

e. ____ black diamond

f. ____ black gold

g. ____ black mark

h. ____ blackjack

i. ____ black widow

j. ____ Blackbeard

k. ____ blackberries

l. ____ black-eyed peas

1. something undesirable on one's record

2. a bruise

3. a tupelo tree

4. really petroleum

5. really coal

6. raven, crow, vulture

7. a pirate flag or a card game

8. a spider

9. a vote to keep a person from joining an organization

10. a pirate

11. a cowpea

12. purple or black edible fruits

What other "black" words can you think of? List them below.

Below draw a "black and white" picture of one of your "black" words.

SMOKEY THE BEAR

On November 9, 1976, Smokey the Bear died. After his rescue from a raging forest fire as a cub, Smokey the Bear was the symbol of the United States' national effort to fight the terrible destruction of our forests by fire. Smokey made his home at the zoo in Washington, D.C., where he made friends with thousands of people.

Smokey had one message for everyone in our country. Solve the puzzle below and find out what it was. Read each pair of words and circle the one that contains the *long vowel*. Then, write the *first* letter of the circled word in the box. Use the letters in the boxes to fill in the blanks at the bottom of the page.

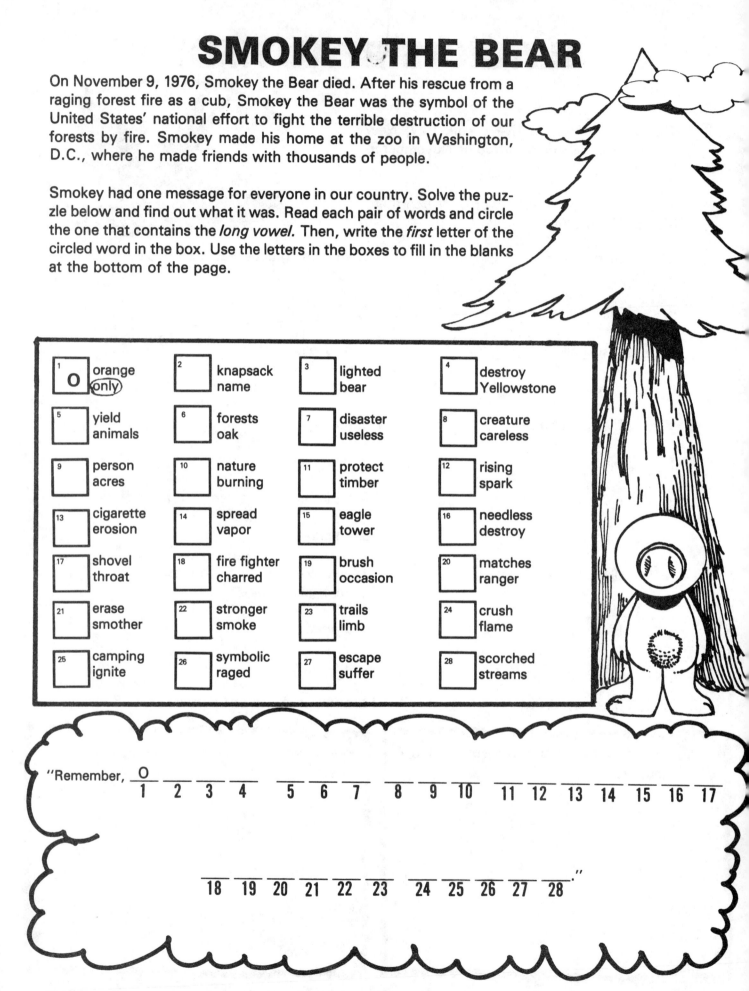

1 **O** orange (only)	2 knapsack name	3 lighted bear	4 destroy Yellowstone
5 yield animals	6 forests oak	7 disaster useless	8 creature careless
9 person acres	10 nature burning	11 protect timber	12 rising spark
13 cigarette erosion	14 spread vapor	15 eagle tower	16 needless destroy
17 shovel throat	18 fire fighter charred	19 brush occasion	20 matches ranger
21 erase smother	22 stronger smoke	23 trails limb	24 crush flame
25 camping ignite	26 symbolic raged	27 escape suffer	28 scorched streams

"Remember, $\underset{1}{\text{O}}$ $\underline{\quad}_{2}$ $\underline{\quad}_{3}$ $\underline{\quad}_{4}$ $\underline{\quad}_{5}$ $\underline{\quad}_{6}$ $\underline{\quad}_{7}$ $\underline{\quad}_{8}$ $\underline{\quad}_{9}$ $\underline{\quad}_{10}$ $\underline{\quad}_{11}$ $\underline{\quad}_{12}$ $\underline{\quad}_{13}$ $\underline{\quad}_{14}$ $\underline{\quad}_{15}$ $\underline{\quad}_{16}$ $\underline{\quad}_{17}$

$\underline{\quad}_{18}$ $\underline{\quad}_{19}$ $\underline{\quad}_{20}$ $\underline{\quad}_{21}$ $\underline{\quad}_{22}$ $\underline{\quad}_{23}$ $\underline{\quad}_{24}$ $\underline{\quad}_{25}$ $\underline{\quad}_{26}$ $\underline{\quad}_{27}$ $\underline{\quad}_{28}$."

A FAMOUS INDIAN

The first poem to win national acclaim was *Song of Hiawatha* by Henry Wadsworth Longfellow. It was published in book form on November 10, 1855, by Ticknor and Fields, Boston, Massachusetts. In four weeks 10,000 copies were sold.

Read the part of this poem given below and answer the questions.

Song of Hiawatha

by Henry Wadsworth Longfellow

By the shores of Gitche Gumee,
By the shining Big-Sea-Water,
Stood the wigwam of Nokomis,
Daughter of the Moon, Nokomis;
Dark behind it rose the forest,
Rose the black and gloomy pine-trees,
Rose the firs with cones upon them;
Bright before it beat the water,
Beat the clear and sunny water,
Beat the shining Big-Sea-Water.

There the wrinkled, old Nokomis
Nursed the little Hiawatha,
Rocked him in his linden cradle,
Bedded soft in moss and rushes,
Safely bound with reindeer sinews;
Stilled his fretful wail by saying,
"Ewa-yeal my little owlet!"
Lulled him into slumber, singing,
"Hush! the Naked Bear will hear thee!
Who is this that lights the wigwam?
With his great eyes lights the wigwam?
Ewa-yeal my little owlet!"

Many things Nokomis taught him
Of the stars that shine in heaven;
Showed him Ishkoodah, the comet,
Ishkoodah, with fiery tresses;
Showed the Death-Dance of the spirits,
Warriors with their plumes and war-clubs,
Flaring far away to northward
In the frosty nights of Winter;
Showed the broad, white road in heaven,
Pathway of the ghosts, the shadows,
Running straight across the heavens,
Crowded with the ghosts, the shadows.

1. Who was Nokomis? _____
   _____

2. Who was Hiawatha? _____ _____
   _____

3. List three adjectives used to describe the pine trees.
   _____, _____, _____

4. List three adjectives used to describe the water.
   _____, _____, _____

5. Give a definition for the word "sinews" as used in line 15.
   _____
   _____

6. Explain the phrase "Stilled his fretful wail" found in line 16.
   _____
   _____

7. What did Nokomis call Hiawatha?
   _____

8. Name one thing Nokomis taught Hiawatha.
   _____
   _____

75

TWINKLE, TWINKLE

A patent was granted to Alvan Clark of Cambridge, Massachusetts, November 11, 1851, for a combination of a glass and a sliding tube. This invention allowed people to view things in the sky that were not visible with the naked eye.

Answer the questions below to find out what this invention is.

Read the sentences. If the italicized word is a verb, circle the letter in the verb column. If the word is a noun, circle the letter in the noun column. Match the sentence number with the letter you circled and write the letter on the correct line below.

		Verb	Noun
1.	The *dog* ate the bone.	z	e
2.	Jeff *swam* in the lake.	o	b
3.	The *car* is dirty.	c	s
4.	All the *houses* need painting.	r	t
5.	Sam *walked* home alone.	p	d
6.	My *grandfather* is coming to visit.	y	e
7.	The *weather* is getting colder.	f	e
8.	I think *planes* are great.	s	l
9.	My neighbor *taught* me how to dance.	c	g

___ ___ ___ ___ ___ ___ ___ ___ ___
 4   1   8   7   3   9   2   5   6

On the back of this sheet, write three sentences using three of the italicized words in the sentences above.

76

VETERANS DAY

Veterans Day honors men and women who have served in the United States armed services. Veterans Day is a legal federal holiday throughout the United States. It is celebrated on November 11. Veterans Day celebrations include parades and speeches. Special services are held at the Tomb of the Unknown Soldier in Arlington National Cemetery, Arlington, Virginia.

Use the chart to fill in the blanks.

	Parades	Speeches	Ceremonies
12:00	Parade-Main Street	Mr. Smith	
1:00			Flag Ceremony
1:30		Mr. Grayman	
2:30			Cemetery Dedication
3:00		Ms. Truman	
3:30			
4:00	Parade-Center St.	General Berg	

1. At 1:30 who will be speaking? _____

2. Main Street parade begins at _____.

3. What time will General Berg speak? _____

4. Cemetery dedication begins at _____.

5. Who will be speaking when the Center Street parade begins? _____

★ ★ ★ ★ ★ ★ ★ ★ ★ ★ ★ ★

Use the chart to make up two more questions for a friend to answer.

77

UP, UP AND AWAY

The first balloon flight to rise higher than 70,000 feet was made on November 11, 1935, by Orvil Anderson and Albert Stevens, both captains in the U.S. Army Air Force. The balloon, the *Explorer II,* started at Rapid City, South Dakota, and flew about 240 miles to White Lake, South Dakota. The flight took eight hours and thirteen minutes.

Read the puzzles below. Choose the correct answers from the balloon ladder and write them on the lines.

1. I am one of the largest statues ever constructed. I hold a torch in my hand. You can climb a stairway inside me. I am the

    _____.

2. While you are driving across me, you can see Alcatraz. You will see the Pacific Ocean under me. I am the _____.

3. I am an extremely deep cavern. You can walk inside of me and see fantastic stalagmites and stalactites. You can visit me in New Mexico. I am the _____.

4. I am a national park located in Arizona. The Colorado River rushes through me. My banks consist of rocks, cliffs, ridges, and hills. I am the _____.

5. I am located in northwestern Wyoming. I am famous for geysers, boiling springs, and petrified forests. I am the _____.

6. A song has been written about me. I was built in London 600 years ago. Later I was reconstructed in Arizona. I am _____.

Statue of Liberty

Carlsbad Caverns

Grand Canyon

Lake Placid

Golden Gate Bridge

Empire State Building

Yellowstone Park

London Bridge

7. I am one of the tallest skyscrapers in the world. I am 102 stories high. You can visit me in New York City. I am the _____.

8. I was the home of the 1980 Winter Olympics. Eric Heiden won five gold medals here. I am located in New York. I am _____.

THERE'S GOLD

The first gold certificates were issued on November 13, 1865. These certificates were used instead of money or gold to pay debts.

Gold has always been a very valuable metal throughout history. Gold has gone up and down in price in recent years from about thirty dollars an ounce to as high as eight-hundred dollars an ounce.

Read the chart to answer the questions below.

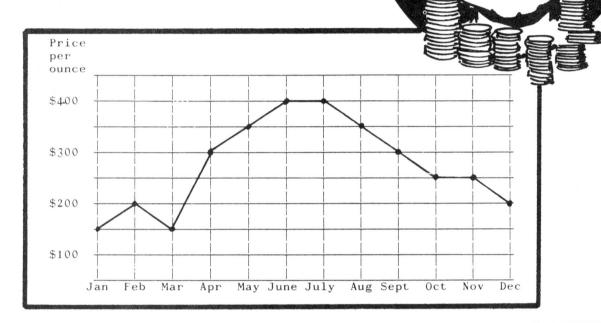

1. What was the price of gold in March? _____

2. What was the price of gold in September? _____

3. Was gold worth more in June than in October? _____

4. What was the total price of gold for both December and February? _____

5. What was the total price of gold for both April and July? _____

6. What two months was gold at $300.00 an ounce? _____

7. What is the price difference of gold in January and December? _____

I HEAR A SYMPHONY

The first full-sized symphony orchestra devoted exclusively to radio broadcasting was formed November 13, 1937. It was the National Broadcasting Company (NBC) Symphony Orchestra. It first played at 10:00 p.m. over the radio stations WEAF and WJZ in New York City.

Use the music secret code to figure out the musical message below. Fill in the correct alphabet letters to match each numeral. It will tell you some important information.

Code:

a	b	c	d	e	f	g	h	i	j	k	l	m
1	2	3	4	5	6	7	8	9	10	11	12	13

n	o	p	q	r	s	t	u	v	w	x	y	z
14	15	16	17	18	19	20	21	22	23	24	25	26

Musical Message:

1 18 20 21 18 15   20 15 19 3 1 14 9 14 9   23 1 19

20 8 5   6 9 18 19 20   3 15 14 4 21 3 20 15 18   15 6

20 8 9 19   19 25 13 16 8 15 14 25   15 18 3 8 5 19 20 18 1

On the back use the music code and write a secret message to a friend.

COLLECTORS' ITEMS

The third Monday in November is the beginning of National Stamp Collecting Week. Many people have different types of collections. Below is a list of items that people collect. However, they are all mixed up. Put them in alphabetical order.

silverware   candles
models   paintings
coins   souvenirs
autographs   paperweights
butterflies   clocks
stamps   pottery
post cards   buttons
dolls   bottles
china   miniatures

_____   _____
_____   _____
_____   _____
_____   _____
_____   _____
_____   _____
_____   _____
_____   _____
_____   _____

List four items that you would like to collect.
_____

If you have a collection, write about it below. Tell how you got started, why you collect these items and where you find them. If you don't have a collection, write about one you would like to have, why you would like it and where you could find your items. You may have to use the back.

_____
_____
_____
_____
_____
_____
_____
_____
_____
_____
_____

"A-MAIZE-ING"

The first corn or maize to be found by British settlers in the New World was discovered on November 16, 1620, in Provincetown, Massachusetts, by a group of sixteen Pilgrims led by Miles Standish and William Bradford. They named the place Corn Hill.

See if you can "a-maize" yourself and match each "corn" vocabulary word to its meaning.

1. corncob   a. _____ the outer covering of the eyeball

2. cornea   b. _____ the horn of plenty, a symbol of a rich harvest

3. corner   c. _____ a musical instrument that looks like a short trumpet

4. cornet   d. _____ the coarse leaves enclosing an ear of corn

5. cornucopia   e. _____ silly or dull because of being old-fashioned

6. cornerstone   f. _____ the center part of an ear of corn

7. cornhusk   g. _____ a heavy molding used along the top of a wall usually for decoration

8. corny   h. _____ the place where two sidewalls meet

9. corncrib   i. _____ the stone that lies at the corner of a building

10. cornice   j. _____ a bin or small building for storing cobs of corn

Write either a "corny" joke or a short "corny" poem. Share it with a friend.

_____

_____

_____

_____

_____

_____

_____

M-I-C-K-E-Y M-O-U-S-E

November 18 is Mickey Mouse's birthday. He first appeared in the animated cartoon called "Steamboat Willie," in 1928. Mickey Mouse is now known and loved all over the world.

Look at the puzzle below. Read the main category on the left side. Complete the puzzle with words that *begin* with the letters of Mickey's name and also fit in the categories.

M I C K E Y

Category	M	I	C	K	E	Y
Noun						
Adjective						
Toy						
Country						

M O U S E

Category	M	O	U	S	E
Noun					
Clothing					
Musical Instrument					
Astronomy					

On the back write a paragraph telling what would be your favorite thing to do if you could spend one day with Mickey Mouse.

SNOWMOBILING

The first snowmobile patent was obtained by Carl J.E. Elason on November 22, 1927. The snowmobile is a motorized sled that carries one or two persons over ice and snow. Snowmobiling is a popular sport in Canada and the northern United States.

It takes a snowmobile thirty minutes to go from the cabin to the forest. Fill in the blanks with the correct times.

	If we leave the cabin at	we will arrive at the forest at
1.	9:00	_____
2.	9:10	_____
3.	10:00	_____
4.	10:15	_____
5.	10:30	_____
6.	11:45	_____
7.	11:05	_____
8.	10:12	_____
9.	11:53	_____
10.	_____	10:00
11.	_____	10:45
12.	_____	11:30

On the back of this sheet, make up three time problems for a friend to solve.

IT'S A RINGER!

The Horseshoe Manufacturing Machine was patented on November 23, 1835, by Henry Burden of Troy, New York. His machine produced a completed horseshoe from a rod of iron that was fed into it. It produced shoes more rapidly and uniformly than the hand production method.

The word horseshoe is two words put together to make a new word. Use the words in the horseshoe to make new words (compound words).

1. _____
2. _____
3. _____
4. _____
5. _____
6. _____
7. _____
8. _____
9. _____
10. _____

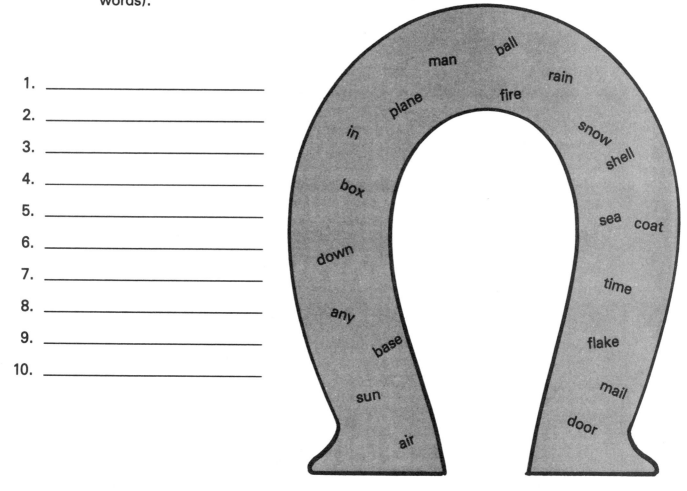

man ball rain fire plane snow in shell box sea coat down time any flake base mail sun door air

On the back of this sheet, write three sentences using compound words.

THANKSGIVING HOMONYMS

BAND OR BANNED ?

Homonyms are words that sound the same but have different meanings and usually different spellings. The following sentences pertain to Thanksgiving. Underline the correct answer.

1. The Pilgrims used an (adds, adze) for planing wood.

2. Pilgrims could brew their own (ale, ail).

3. Samoset said he would meet the governor by the sandy (beech, beach).

4. Mrs. Bradford made (bread, bred) from cornmeal.

5. Indians stored extra food in their (cache, cash).

6. The early Pilgrims could dry (carets, carrots).

7. Priscilla sent her husband out for a (chord, cord) of wood.

8. At first the women had to wash their clothes in the (creek, creak).

9. Our pet fawn was (done, dun) in color.

10. The (dough, doe) was grayish-brown also.

11. One of the enemies of the pioneers was the (lynx, links).

12. Indians called their corn (May's, maze, maize).

13. Deer (mete, meet, meat) was made into jerky.

14. Did they have to (pare, pair, pear) the fruit before drying it?

15. Squanto used a (real, reel) in an expert manner.

16. The Indians planted their maize in (roes, rows).

17. The bowstring was (taut, tot, taught).

You may want to make up your own homonym sentences. Use the back of this sheet.

MAIZE OR MAZE ?

PARE OR PEAR ?

DON'T FENCE ME IN!

On November 24, 1874, J.F. Glidden patented a new type of fencing called the barbed wire. He twisted two strands of wire together and tied a short piece of wire between the twists. Cattle were afraid of the barbed wire. This new type of wire signaled the end of the free American range.

Look at the lengths of barbed wire below. Measure each with a standard ruler. Place the mixed fraction in the *box.* Next count the barbs and place that numeral in the *circle* provided. Multiply the fraction times the number of barbs and put your answer on the line.

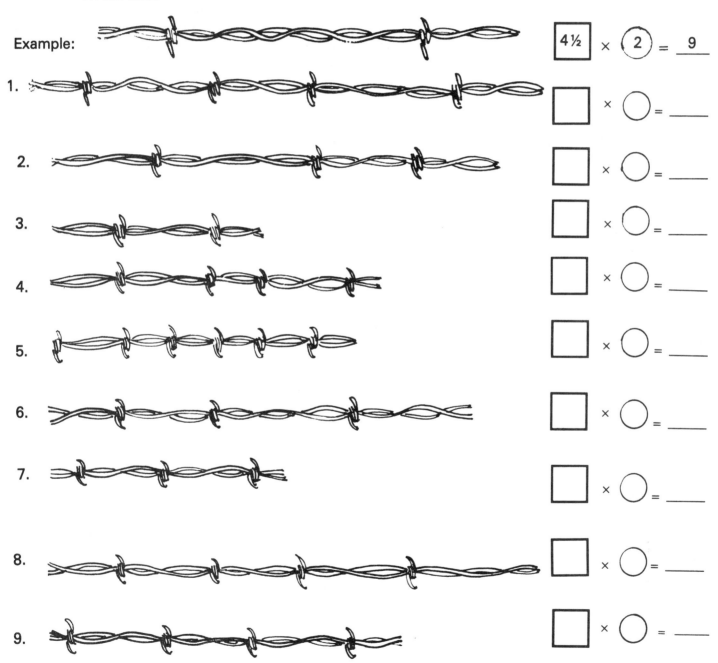

Example: $4\frac{1}{2}$ × ② = __9__

1. ☐ × ◯ = ____

2. ☐ × ◯ = ____

3. ☐ × ◯ = ____

4. ☐ × ◯ = ____

5. ☐ × ◯ = ____

6. ☐ × ◯ = ____

7. ☐ × ◯ = ____

8. ☐ × ◯ = ____

9. ☐ × ◯ = ____

A POWWOW

November 25 is National Indian Heritage Day. Native Americans were in this country long before any "white" man came over. Many false statements are made about all Indians. Below is a list of different tribes of Indians. Choose one and research it by using an encyclopedia. Write a report below; include facts about types of housing, clothing, food, the part of the country they live in, customs and any other information you feel is important.

Apache	Aztec	Algonquin	Blackfoot
Chinook	Cree	Crow	Cheyenne
Comanche	Erie	Fox	Hopi
Huron	Iroquois	Inca	Iowa
Kansas	Kiowa	Lumbee	Maya
Mohawk	Narraganset	Navaho	Omaha
Osage	Oneida	Ottawa	Olmec
Pawnee	Paiute	Pima	Potawatomi
Quapaw	Seneca	Shoshoni	Shawnee
Seminole	Sioux	Tuscarora	Toltec
Tupi	Teton	Ute	Xinca
Yuma	Zuni		

_____

_____

_____

_____

_____

_____

_____

_____

_____

_____

_____

_____

Have you ever seen skywriting? The first skywriting was held at noontime over Times Square, New York City on November 28, 1922. A captain from the Royal Air Force spelled out in letters a half mile high at a 10,000 foot altitude the message, "Hello, U.S.A. Call Vanderbilt 7200."

Work the problems to find out the name of this famous man.

1. 610
   × 5
   ———
   3050

2. 533
   × 4
   ———

3. 202
   × 7
   ———

4. 600
   × 6
   ———

5. 942
   × 3
   ———

6. 811
   × 2
   ———

7. 722
   × 4
   ———

8. 711
   × 6
   ———

9. 201
   × 8
   ———

10. 632
    × 3
    ———

11. 911
    × 1
    ———

C
— — — — —   — — — — — —
1 2 3 4 5   6 7 8 9 10 11

On the back of this sheet, make up five more problems for a friend to solve.

	B	C	D
1.	○ 3150	● 3050	○ 3005
	w	y	z
2.	○ 2223	○ 2132	○ 2032
	r	s	t
3.	○ 1414	○ 1514	○ 1415
	j	k	i
4.	○ 3066	○ 3666	○ 3600
	l	m	n
5.	○ 2826	○ 2926	○ 2906
	R	T	S
6.	○ 1642	○ 1622	○ 1623
	T	u	v
7.	○ 2908	○ 2888	○ 2988
	r	s	t
8.	○ 4266	○ 4265	○ 4366
	m	n	o
9.	○ 1688	○ 1608	○ 1618
	D	F	e
10.	○ 1969	○ 1869	○ 1896
	l	r	k
11.	○ 921	○ 911	○ 922

LET'S BUILD PYRAMIDS

November 29, 1922, is the day that King Tutankhamen's tomb was discovered in Egypt. Lord Carnarvon of England and Howard Carter discovered the tomb filled with many, many treasures. Egyptians used to build pyramids to honor their rulers. They also buried their kings with great treasures of jewelry, food, clothing, furniture and other things they thought he might need for a happy afterlife. Pyramids were very large buildings. It took thousands of slaves many, many years to build these magnificent strong structures. They have lasted more than 4,000 years.

Below build word pyramids of your own. Start at the top of the pyramid and work down as far as you can go. Notice that once you've used a word you may not drop it from the pyramid. An example of a Thanksgiving pyramid is given.

Pilgrims
many Pilgrims
many English Pilgrims
many friendly English Pilgrims
many hardworking, friendly, English Pilgrims
many strong, hardworking, friendly, English Pilgrims

ANSWER KEY

September

EGGSACTLY WHERE AM I?   Page 5
Answers will vary.
1. dairy—milk and cheese
2. fruits and vegetables
3. breads and cereals
4. meats

1. France
2. Brazil
3. Italy
4. Poland
5. Austria
6. Spain
7. China
8. Indiana
9. Ireland
10. Sweden

DON'T BE IN THE DOGHOUSE   Page 6
1. 3   6. 6
2. 5   7. 9
3. 8   8. 7
4. 10   9. 1
5. 2   10. 4

A REST DAY   Page 7
Answers will vary.

DIAL "O" FOR OPERATOR   Page 8
Answers will vary.

CLOWNING AROUND   Page 9
Answers will vary.

EXTRA! EXTRA!   Page 10
1. to draw out by effort
2. very unusual, remarkable
3. perception that occurs in addition to the normal senses
4. going beyond reasonable limits
5. not part of the regular course of study but under supervision of the school
6. to turn over to the jurisdiction of another country, state, etc.
7. a spectacular, elaborate theatrical production
8. outside the earth; from another planet

"SAY CHEESE!"   Page 11
1. twice a month
2. not legal
3. substance with low freezing point
4. noon—middle of the day
5. self-signature
6. two-wheel vehicle
7. not able to read or write
8. the ground in front
9. the life story about one's self
10. the middle of the air
11. against war
12. the extreme front

FILL 'ER UP!   Page 12
2. $18.00 $15.36   6. $8.40 $21.76
3. 14.40   25.60   7. 2.40   16.64
4. 3.60   3.84   8. 24.00   32.00
5. 10.80   7.68   9. 30.00   8.96
                10. 25.20   11.52

KEEP ON PEDALING   Page 13
2. 90 miles, 6 hrs.   4. 75 miles, 5 hrs.
3. 30 miles, 2 hrs.   5. 105 miles, 7 hrs.
                     6. 75 miles, 5 hrs.

A CLAY PIGEON   Page 14
Answers will vary.

A RIDE IN RHODE ISLAND   Page 15
1. 1972   4. 160 mph
2. 150 mph   5. 165 mph
3. 165 mph   6. 5 mph, 15 mph
              7. 1950

I PLEDGE ALLEGIANCE . . .   Page 16
I pledge allegiance to the flag of the United States of America and to the Republic for which it stands, one Nation under God, indivisible, with liberty and justice for all.

CALIFORNIA, HERE WE COME
                             Page 17
Answers will vary.

THE LOG ROLLED OVER   Page 18
2. Are you backing out?
3. She was very angry!
4. He is very clumsy.
5. He causes me trouble!
6. I'm very healthy.
7. Don't get mad!
8. Be brave.
9. Slow down!
10. Is Dad ever feeling sad.
11. He lost a lot of money on that deal.
12. Don't cry over past mistakes.

STAR-SPANGLED WORDS   Page 19
1. a flash or beam of light
2. dangerous
3. time just after or just before sunset
4. greeted, saluted
5. brave and noble
6. glittered; covered with shiny bright objects
7. flag
8. a wall surrounding the fort
9. a strong light
10. waving; floating

A HERSHEY CRUNCH   Page 20
Answers will vary.

IT'S A BABY . . . .   Page 21
1. 20   3. 6
2. 60   4. 20
           5. 10

SEWING AROUND   Page 22
The Issac Singer Sewing Machine Company

CONSTITUTION WEEK   Page 23
Answers will vary.

SPRINKLE, SPRINKLE   Page 24
Answers will vary.

TENNIS TALK   Page 25
The following words should be circled: bounce, grip, lob, rally, score, serve, slam, slice, volley

A RECIPE FOR FALL   Page 26
Answers will vary.

SEPARATE YOUR FACTS   Page 27
1. fact   9. opinion
2. opinion   10. opinion
3. fact   11. fact
4. opinion   12. opinion
5. opinion   13. fact
6. opinion   14. fact
7. opinion   15. opinion
8. fact

CHOO! CHOO! ALL ABOARD   Page 28
Answers will vary.

TOUCHDOWN!   Page 29
1. 25 yard line   5. 18 points
2. 40 yard line   36 points
3. 20 yards   30 points
4. 25 yards

SLOCUM'S PIN STICKER   Page 30
1. buttonhole   7. skateboard
2. pocketknife   8. dishrag
3. lighthouse   9. somebody
4. wastebasket   10. sunrise
5. grandmother   11. popcorn
6. horseshoe   12. waterhole

October

DEAR DIARY — Page 35

Authors born in October include: Oscar Wilde, e.e. cummings, Geoffrey Chaucer, John Keats, Emily Post, James Whitcomb Riley.

COLOR ME RED — Page 36

1. black
2. orange
3. green
4. red
5. brown
6. purple
7. yellow
8. blue

TAKE GOOD CARE OF YOURSELF — Page 37

Answers will vary.

ITS FIRST BROADCAST — Page 38

1. strike
2. base
3. foul
4. ball
5. home run
6. dugout
7. pitcher
8. shortstop
9. coach
10. world series

HICKORY, DICKORY DOCK — Page 39

1. 12
2. 24
3. 365
4. 60

1. 9:41
2. 8:02
3. 7:12
4. 3:41

5. 11:07
6. 9:26
7. 5:47
8. 12:34

HOW NOW BROWN COW — Page 40

1. Mrs. O'Leary's cow
2. in the barn at 137 Dekoven Street
3. on the evening of October 8, 1871
4. The cow kicked over a lantern in a barn. The fire spread over 21,000 acres causing about $196,000,000 damage. At least three hundred people died, over 90,000 were left homeless.
5. Answers will vary.

A STRIKE AND A SPARE — Page 41

1. Joan
2. 303
3. 583
4. Bill
5. Tim
6. 175
7. 54
8. 751
9. 21, 36, 59, 70, 91, 114, 129, 150, 153, 164

ABSOLUTELY ACCURATE — Page 42

There are over 1900 correct answers.

A NICE BIRTHDAY PRESENT — Page 43

Answers will vary.

LOOK INTO THE FUTURE — Page 44

Answers will vary.

DID YOU HEAR THAT? — Page 45

1. 27
2. 99
3. 40
4. 258
5. 741
6. 253
7. 2,160
8. 64
9. 296
10. 100

ARE YOU A POET, AND DON'T KNOW IT? — Page 46

Answers will vary.

LET'S GO TO SKI SCHOOL — Page 47

1. 417
2. 769
3. 214
4. 546
5. 225
6. 899
7. 99

REACH OUT, REACH OUT... — Page 48

1. $1.96
2. 3.46
3. 5.22
4. 2.29
5. 5.16

OUR FAMOUS LADY — Page 49

1. brazen
2. beacon
3. command
4. ancient
5. yearning
6. astride
7. imprisoned

France gave the statue as a symbol of friendship and to celebrate the hundredth birthday of the United States.

WHAT A SHOCK! — Page 50

OLD IRONSIDES — Page 51

2. 130 ft.
3. 110 ft.
4. 30 ft.
5. 120 ft.
6. 150 ft.
7. 100 ft.
Total: 720 ft.

"ROLL OUT THE BARREL" — Page 52

Answers will vary.

"LET THERE BE PEACE ON EARTH" — Page 53

Answers will vary.

"CLINTON'S DITCH" — Page 54

1. Answers will vary.
2. Grand Canal (China) and parts of canal between Nile and Red Sea.

1. New York State Barge Canal
2. Panama Canal
3. Manchester Canal
4. Suez Canal

SUB POWER — Page 55

1. submarine
2. subtract
3. subway
4. suburb
5. substitute
6. submerge
7. substance
8. subfreezing
9. submit
10. subdivide
11. subsoil
12. subdue

FINGERPRINTS TALK! — Page 56

Answers will vary.

PROJECT CIRRUS — Page 57

1. bush — squirrel — mountain
2. buttercup — raccoon — gully
3. grasses — moose — ditch
4. trees — hare — valley
5. fern — fox — logs
6. ivy — doe
7. moss — bear
8. — buck

THE CARD TIME RECORDER — Page 58

1. 39 ½
2. $197.50
3. $112.50
4. James
5. $ 45.00
6. $370.00
7. $210.00
8. $382.50

THE BATTLE-BORN STATE — Page 59

1. no
2. yes
3. yes
4. yes
5. no
6. yes
7. no
8. yes

Las Vegas

THE MAGIC E! — Page 60

2. twine — twin
3. code — cod
4. spine — spine
5. slime — slim
6. mare — mare
7. cube — cub
8. gale — gal
9. globe — globe
10. scare — scare
11. Answers will vary.

November

CATS FOR ALL SEASONS — Page 65

a. 6
b. 14
c. 1
d. 13
e. 2
f. 5
g. 4
h. 12
i. 15
j. 3
k. 16
l. 9
m. 7
n. 11
o. 8
p. 10

A CHANGE IN THE WEATHER — Page 66

1. F
2. F
3. M
4. M
5. F
6. F
7. F
8. M
9. F
10. M
11. M
12. M
13. F
14. M
15. F
16. F
17. M
18. M
19. F
20. M

21. Answers will vary.

A FAMOUS PIONEER — Page 67

D = 4018
E = 2248
O = 4851
E = 1752
O = 441
N = 294
L = 522
I = 280
A = 776
N = 2877

DANIEL BOONE